GW00642786

CEASE AND DESIST

CEASE AND DESIST

Surviving the Might of the Largest Entertainment
Corporation in the World

Denise Fitzpatrick
with Terry Prone

MERCIER PRESS

MERCIER PRESS
Douglas Village, Cork, Ireland
www.mercierpress.ie

Trade enquiries to Columba Mercier Distribution,
55a Spruce Avenue, Stillorgan Industrial Park, Blackrock, Dublin

© Denise Fitzpatrick, 2006

ISBN 1 85635 491 1

10 9 8 7 6 5 4 3 2 1

Mercier Press receives financial assistance from
the Arts Council/An Chomhairle Ealaíon

This book is sold subject to the condition that it shall not, by way of trade
or otherwise, be lent, resold, hired out or otherwise circulated without the
publisher's prior consent in any form of binding or cover other than that in
which it is published and without a similar condition being imposed on the
subsequent purchaser.

Printed in the EU

CONTENTS

To the many heroic mums and dads like me
who stumbled and occasionally fell
while following their dreams.

Everyone has a TV series, book or film in them. Or so goes the popular myth. This book is about one of the few people who not only took childhood memories and wove them into stories worth filming, but who succeeded against incredible odds and survived to tell the tale.

Denise Fitzpatrick's stories from her earliest years in Ireland of her pet pig have ended up as a twenty-six episode series: Jakers – the Adventures of Piggley Winks, broadcast coast-to-coast in the US to critical acclaim.

Denise's story is passionate, heartwarming, funny, sometimes sad. In Cease and Desist, Denise tells the inside story of how she had to fight against people who tried to destroy her dream, and how she took on Disney, the largest leisure corporation in the world.

Born in 1965 on the Hill of Tara where the high kings of Ireland lived, Denise Fitzpatrick's childhood was filled with carefree fun, fairies, leprechauns and her beloved Raloo Farm. It was in this enchanting environment that her imagination created a storytelling character named Piggley, based on her adorable pet pig. When Denise herself became a mother, she shared her stories with her children. Her lawyer husband, Francis, was fascinated by them. The young couple developed an impossible dream: to bring Piggley to world television. And they did it. They did it while raising a daughter and three sons. They did it against big money, when they had none of their own.

When Denise first started to spin the yarns that would eventually bring Celtic mythology, in fascinating form, to children watching TV half a world away, she had no idea of the grim and sometimes frightening times that lay ahead. Through it all, the Fitzpatricks developed new strengths and deepened their commitment to each other.

From the glamour of the Cannes TV festival to the sheer terror of having to beg your bank to give you one more day before they pull the plug – hers is a story that every entrepreneur has experienced: a rollercoaster from start to finish. The massive financial strains played havoc with their emotions. Constant pleas from concerned family and friends to give up were tempting, but ultimately not persuasive, to a Meath girl with no background in international showbusiness but who was learning – and learning fast – how to deal with film producers, entertainment financiers, top ranking lawyers, accountants and corporation CEOs.

She dealt with them. And she won. This book tells the riveting story of how she did it, the fears she faced and the lessons she learned. Denise Fitzpatrick is a storyteller who takes ancient myths and spins them into fairytales for children. But this book is not a fairytale. It's about the importance of dreams and the value of families. It's dedicated to those who want to believe their dreams can come true. It proves that the small guy sometimes wins.

— Terry Prone

Chapter One

SHOWDOWN IN BOSTON

The worst moment happens in the Algonquin Club in Boston in March 2001. Nothing wrong with the room itself. Nice old furniture. Reasonably cosy.

The two of us have just had dinner with the head of an Italian animation company who wants to buy into Piggley Pooh, the character I invented, based on the piglets on my grandmother's farm. It's a solid offer. A breakthrough to the future.

Except for the Disney Factor. The Disney Factor is what happens when the biggest entertainment corporation in the world decides that a couple of nobodies from Ireland constitute a threat to its billion-dollar operation. That's what happened to Francis, my husband, and me.

I'd invented a children's story character named Piggley Pooh. 'Piggley', because he was a pig. 'Pooh', because it's the Irish reaction to a bad smell and pigs smell! The alliteration worked. More to the point, when you read a Piggley Pooh story aloud to a child, they never forgot what the pig was called. It was a great name.

Until Disney decided it was too close to Winnie the Pooh. Although Disney hadn't created Winnie the Pooh, they had bought the brand from the estate of its creator, A. A. Milne, and had grown the brand brilliantly so that it now generated multi-billion clothing and merchandise earnings all over the world. Now, you might think that Denise and Francis Fitzpatrick from Skryne Hill, County Meath, Ireland could not threaten Disney's continued Winnie the Pooh profitability

…hat's not the way Michael

…is, they went ballistic. Their
…ed on us like vultures. We
…er mind the years of creativity
…ought Piggley Pooh from a pet
…er in a TV pilot. Never mind the
…done by two novices in the TV
…acter a break on the small screen.

Disney…us, so they underestimated the fight
in us. By the time…d reached the Algonquin Club in Boston, we'd fought them in courts all over the world – and in the court of public opinion. We were the young Irish couple taking on the multinational giant. We were David, they were Goliath. We were loved by the animation industry as brave little dreamers refusing to back down in the face of what looked like monied, monopolistic intimidation dressed up as brand-protection.

But we were also weary. Weary of the scale of the battle. No matter what we did or how honestly we argued our case for a little character that had been in my mind from my toddler years, we had the sense that Disney could always find another angle, another way to crush us and our hopes.

Battling a giant is the stuff of myths and movies – not of motherhood. By the time we were fidgeting our way around the small Algonquin Club bedroom, I had four children who had less than no interest in us fighting with the Disney corporation or being away from home as often as that fight required. My husband, Francis, and I were in debt up to our armpits. We were exhausted.

Negotiations with Disney had reached the point where they were offering us $500,000 to abandon the Piggley Pooh name and go away. $500,000 would have been a defeat, but it would at least have allowed us to avoid bankruptcy and go on. We would have lost Piggley Pooh but we would have paid off a lot of our debts and Francis could have come back to Dublin and started a fledgling legal practice again.

The Italian animator with whom we had just dined liked our character so much that he was prepared to make movies around it without calling it Piggley Pooh. He was urging us to settle with Disney so he could have free run with the piglet character. All the way back to the Club in his 4x4, he was insistent that we make the call, get things ironed out and let him get on with animating Piggley Pooh – or whatever Piggley Pooh would have to be called after surrender to Disney. When he parted with us at about nine o'clock, having subjected us to a benign battering of advice, my husband had smiled and nodded: 'OK, Ricki, I hear you: now's the time to surrender and see what we can make of the settlement. You don't need to say another word, Ricki, I'm there. Consider it done. Soon as we get settled, I'll make that phonecall to Disney and take the medicine.'

Because of the time difference in California, we figure the Disney man, Steve Ackerman, will be in his office, even though it's dark outside in Boston. I make encouraging noises at Francis: 'We've nothing to lose at this point. We've taken it as far as we can. Now, we just want enough of a settlement to get out of debt. Just put the call in.'

Francis walks around the room for a bit. Anything but make the final surrender. Especially to Steve Ackerman, who is their chief counsel worldwide. Ackerman is a tough negotiator whose idea of a pleasant introduction is to start off the conversation with 'Francis, you're the bad guy, you're the robber. You're stealing our name, our goodwill, our reputation.' Francis dreads the cold hostility and contempt he meets every time he talks to Ackerman. But he knows there is no putting this one off, so he sits on the edge of the bed and dials the number. He gets through immediately to

Ackerman's assistant: 'Steve isn't available, right now,' she says. 'Let me take your details and I'll get him to call you back.'

This is the worst possible outcome. Francis has steeled himself for nothing. When Ackerman rings back – assuming he does ring back – the initiative's going to be with him. The ball's going to be in his court. Francis looks down at the slightly old-fashioned phone with a hatred it doesn't deserve.

'They probably won't come back to us tonight,' I say, because there's no point in the two of us sitting watching the phone. We talk about Mondo, Ricki's company. And how they're offering us an advance of a quarter of a million. So, if we can get something decent out of Disney, say $500,000, we'll have $750,000. It's not great but it's a hell of a lot better than nothing.

'I wonder if we could get $1m from Disney,' I ask out loud. 'You only get $1m by asking for $2m, so maybe you should –'

'Maybe we should get real, here,' Francis says. 'This is not some weekend poker game we're playing among friends. This is Michael Eisner's Disney corporation and they have us between a rock and a hard place.'

I stay silent. I can see the pressure Francis is feeling, but I know that it would drive him absolutely crazy if I mention it. Francis is an Irish lawyer coming fast up the intellectual rights learning curve, trying to sew up a deal with an Italian company, trying to negotiate with Disney. He has a case against Disney in the European Courts. For the two of us, this is a life and death issue, but he knows that for Disney, we are simply a nuisance. A nuisance without urgency: they know damn well that film-makers, whether in Italy or Ireland, the US or Japan, won't move on our project, no matter how much they like it, as long as the pitch is queered by the legal threats of the Disney corporation. Denise and Francis Fitzpatrick and Piggley Pooh aren't going anywhere fast.

On the other hand, we have caused that big corporation

to lose the copyright case they'd taken against us in Japan; in America, Disney were too late to file an objection so we were registered owners; *and* the European decision wasn't in at that point. Europe is a big play for Disney because it is the first full hearing of the case. The other two – Japan and America – were more pre-trial victories. Hollow victories in a sense but still victories. But in Europe, they have mustered their top lawyers and trademark agents in London. They are on the ball this time.

'Small guys don't win against big corporations, that's the reality,' Francis says, summing it all up for me. 'We've got a good case from a legal point of view but the reality is there are very few individuals who would beat a big corporation. So we've got to –'

He's interrupted by the phone.

Francis leaps at it, eager to get it over with. I lean over to hear the conversation, but stay put, in an armchair across the room. Francis doesn't need me crowding him.

'Hi, this is Steve here.'

'Oh Steve, how are you?'

'Francis, you were looking for me, what do you want?'

Terse. Brusque. Can't even waste the time on civility.

Francis remembers twelve years earlier, when Adrian Hardiman, now a judge in Ireland's Supreme Court, was acting as a barrister for Francis in a case. Standing up before Judge Moriarty, Hardiman made a lovely opening statement to the effect of 'in the words of Cromwell, this has gone on far too long to do anyone any good'.

Now, seated in the Algonquin, Francis quotes Hardiman/Cromwell to Ackerman, who gets even more impatient.

'What do you mean?'

'Steve, you know, we could settle this matter rather than have the court decide for us.'

'Francis, you're the one who has taken our name, you're

the one who has robbed us, we can settle, sure – but we're only going to pay a few thousand. That's all this is worth to us.'

'Well, Steve, what figure are we actually looking at? What precisely would you be prepared to pay?'

'Francis, let's not go over old ground, you know you once demanded twenty million. If you want to go there, we have nothing to discuss. If you're ready to be reasonable about it, then we do have a settlement.'

No persuasion. No respect for a vanquished foe. Francis and I are clearly no more than debris from a battle and the issue is how cheaply we can be swept up. Francis takes a deep breath.

'Steve, I will be reasonable about it,' he says. 'I do want to settle and there's no point in going any further.'

Not if we want our children to eat, I think. Not if we want to pay our debts to the friends and relatives who have trusted us with their hard-earned money in one loan after another.

'We have the power to settle this tonight.'

It's about the only power we have, Francis. But go on, flex our non-existent muscle at him – before we lie down and let him roll over us.

'My wife is with me here and we're the decision-makers.'

That's right. Put us together, you get two white flags, four hands in the air.

'And I'm sure you can get your instructions.'

Even from a distance of several feet, I hear Ackerman's resentful grunt in response to one of Francis' favourite negotiating tactics with him: pointing out that while Francis and I are the bosses, Ackerman is a functionary who always has to take his instructions from Michael Eisner. Francis' repeated reminders of this didn't sit well with Ackerman. But it was a good way of putting him slightly off his stroke, and when you're on the losing, little guy side of an argument, waiting for the giant fist to come down and crush you like an insect, you'll use anything that will put the giant on the back foot.

Steve Ackerman responds to Francis' dig by saying yeah, he could get instructions. In fact, he wouldn't have to go to get them. He already had them. The prospect of acting on those instructions gets him into better humour. One notch away from cordiality, he is. Francis takes another deep breath. But quietly, not wanting to give any clues to the pressure, the sense of defeat.

'Well, listen, Steve,' he says, with forced brightness, 'why don't you look at your instructions and see if you can settle tonight and phone me back and I'll do the deal with you.'

'Yeah,' he says. 'That'd be good.'

'The other problem I have, Steve –' Francis hesitates.

His hesitation meets silence from the other end. The message of that silence: 'Your problem is your problem.' But Francis doggedly ploughs on, one hand over his eyes as he concentrates. You need to concentrate when you're working out how far into the dust the other guy is going to grind you.

'We've incurred a lot of costs. You know, those costs really should be separate from the damages –'

'*Damages?*'

'Well, whatever you call the recompense you're going to need to pay us to give up the Piggley Pooh name –'

Ackerman hits the roof. No matter how badly he wants to get rid of this irksome Irish couple with their ridiculous children's pig character, he can't resist rising to the annoyance implicit in the suggestion that in some way his corporation owes the Fitzpatricks damages. Francis holds the phone a little way from his ear to preserve his ear drum as Ackerman goes back into the old routine, like a singer comfortable with the chorus of a song. I hear every word now. Not that I need to. I could sing this song right along with him, I've heard it so often.

17

'Francis, be in no doubt. You are the author of your own misfortune. You and your wife brought this case on your-selves. You and your wife are setting out to steal our name, our character, our brand, our investment. You and your wife are thieves. Irish thieves. Have been from the word go.'

I'm waiting for him to mention our children. Twice. Not in any affectionate, let's-bond-about-the-kids way. In a deeply threatening, personal way. That's what he'd done the first time he'd met Francis. Got the image of our children into their father's head, then promised to go after Francis world-wide. Probably bankrupt him. So that the children he had just mentioned would not be able to go to a decent school. The first time Ackerman said it, at that initial meeting, Francis was flummoxed. He couldn't quite believe what he'd heard.

When Ackerman hammered home the promise of action against us and its implications for our children, Francis had gone berserk. He lost control. Now losing control is a fatal mistake for a lawyer but as a human being it's just a natural, atavistic reaction. Your kids are being threatened. At that first meeting in Burbank, Francis jumped up and roared, matching profanities and threats. I wasn't there. Thank God. I don't need to be around when my husband threatens to kill perfect strangers. He doesn't do it a lot. But in that opening foray, it had caused Ackerman to back down and plead for everyone to keep their cool.

Now, however, on this long-distance phonecall, Acker-man says nothing about our children. Just about us. Up close, personal and insulting, he gets, but just about Francis and me. Particularly Francis.

I find myself getting out of the armchair without knowing what I plan to do. Not that it matters. Francis doesn't see me moving. He's so focused, it's obvious he can *see* Ackerman in front of him. Not a pretty sight, I think. Ackerman looks like a hardened version of Elton John. With less hair. Yes, I know Elton's isn't real, but Ackerman doesn't even have a hair piece.

Francis is polite by nature. But if someone gets personally nasty, he can respond in kind. As he does now.

'Listen, I'm the president of a corporation,' he yells. 'It may only be a small corporation but it still is a corporation and I'm its president. You're only a fucking lawyer, remember that.'

I sit down again. Francis needs no help from me in the invective department. Although I'm willing. And qualified: after all, I'm the vice-president of this magnificent corporation. A corporation of two, based in Meath.

'And another thing,' Francis adds. 'I insist on speaking to Eisner. As part of this settlement, I want to talk to Eisner myself. You can bloody well tell him that. He's going to pick up the phone to me. It's about time I was addressed by the president.'

Then both of them realise there's no point in yelling at each other across a continent. They are wasting each other's time. Francis calms down and reiterates the need to get the issue settled once and for all, suggesting that Ackerman phone his ultimate boss, Michael Eisner, and talk to him.

'You know that we can make a decision tonight,' Francis says. 'Come back to us. The issue of costs has to be dealt with because despite me being the author of my own misfortune, there's a misfortune of costs here that have to be paid.'

'If you settle this, Francis, I'll talk to Eisner and see if he'll speak to you.'

'Yeah, OK, phone me back then, talk to Eisner.'

Francis puts down the phone and breathes a long out-breath as if he has been saving air for a month. He's flustered, adrenalin pumping right through him, giving him a red face. I do a 'well done Francis' and the two of us walk around that small room like two caged animals, Francis talking out loud, half to me, half to himself.

'Right, these guys are going to phone us back, we've got to have some plans here because if we're going to settle, now is the time, it will never come again, believe you me as a lawyer. This is the time to settle because there won't be another opportunity. The judgement is coming out in Europe in a couple of weeks. We are in control of our destiny now but if we don't settle, the judge is in control of our destiny. We may get a good decision, we may not. You're always better to take the certainty. Take the decision now, let's control it.'

'If we settle tonight, how much are we going to get?' I ask.

'I don't think they want to offer us more than half a million. We've got to meet somewhere in the middle.'

In the middle of what, I wonder? If we could get a million, we'd be foolish not to take it, pay our debts, get the banks back on side, go back to Francis' law practice and get out of this hell. When Ackerman comes back on the line, Francis should just take whatever he can, even if it's as low as half a million. Anything, just to get a settlement and get back to real life after five years of hell.

And it had been hell. In all our dealings with them, whenever we were in Burbank or whenever we had a letter from them or sent them a letter, they always played the game on their terms. Reduce, revise, revisit. It was like a parody of that environmental slogan: 'Reduce, re-re-use and recycle.' They were a big corporation, they could let us bleed to death. Commonsense dictated that we couldn't go on another minute, never mind another three months or six months.

I've never been a big lover of commonsense and so, while nodding at every point being made to me, and accepting that surrender is inevitable, inside I'm disappointed. My dreams are dying. My character, Piggley Pooh, is finished.

My hopes and aspirations slipping through my open fingers. The disappointment is massive, but I make the noises of being resigned to defeat. As the negotiator, Francis wants to know how far those noises go. Are we going to take whatever they offer and run?

'No,' I say, suddenly firm. 'We don't have much, but we do have our dignity. They're not taking that away from us. So we're going to see if they'll pay our costs and if they don't, well, we're going to tell them get lost.'

Francis is still looking at me, surprised and half-smiling, when the phone rings again.

This time, he doesn't leap for it. Instead, he's quite relaxed. Sweet surrender. All Disney have to do at this point is be civilised. Francis lifts the phone.

When Ackerman's assistant puts him through, it sounds as if he, too, has gone through an attitude-change process parallel to our own. He's in good form. In fact, he is quite animated: 'Hi Francis, listen, settlement's on, we can pay you, we've agreed to pay you, I've spoken to Eisner. He is going to speak to you so I know you'll be delighted with that.'

Francis looks across at me for a long moment. Then he winks. Winks? Then he begins to respond in a low, defeated tone of voice. His eyes are twinkling madly, but his voice sounds like he's terminally depressed.

'Yeah, Steve. I am delighted. Thank you very much. I appreciate that. Indeed, I appreciate all your efforts. But we do still have this major problem on costs.'

'Oh yeah.' Ackerman is like a guy kicking a small grain of sand out of his shoe. 'Tell ya what, Francis, we are taking a strong line on this. Disney are not going to pay your costs because you brought the action on yourselves, you did create your own misfortune so we're going to pay you a reasonable sum and we've spoken about that.'

21

There it is. The bottom line. Perhaps $500,000 to go away and let the Disney wrecking ball reduce a lifetime's work to smithereens.

'Look Steve,' Francis says, his voice grey and dull: dead man talking. 'You're giving me very little room here. I did tell you before you spoke to Eisner that costs was a major issue for me because the sort of money you're talking about doesn't pay my bills. I've spent almost a million on this, maybe more, I can't tell you. And the money alone doesn't address the time – look at all the time I've taken away from my profession on this. I've spent five years of my life, I need something.'

'No, Francis, no. That's it, take it or leave it. No costs. Let's talk about the settlement sum.'

Francis lets a long silence fall. The other guy doesn't fill it. My husband rubs his face with his hand. But there's no tension in the gesture. He seems totally relaxed. I can make neither head nor tail of it.

'Steve, you and me have said a lot of things to each other that I'm not proud of,' Francis murmurs. Ackerman's little voice comes quacking out of the telephone handset. He's being quite magnanimous, now he's in the home straight, saying that both sides had insulted each other in inappropriate ways, but that whatever had been said, had been said in the heat of battle and would now be forgotten.

'Steve, that's very generous of you,' Francis responds. 'I'd like to think that the next time you're in Dublin or I'm in LA we'll get together and we'll have a beer or two and start again.'

Ackerman allows that this beer might be a good thing, but indicates that he has the board of Disney waiting for a conclusion on this issue. Message: cut to the chase, you miserable Irish thief and tell us you're settling for $500,000. Not a penny more, not a penny less. The excitement of impending closure makes his voice practically vibrate. Another one bites the dust. In this case, an Irish animated piglet. Piggley Pooh's snout is squashed flat, his creator (me) squashed just as flat, and our defender, Francis, finally folding the tent. Although he sees us as minor, our defeat is nonetheless a big deal for him because he can now march into his board and say 'Problem solved, Winnie the Pooh is saved, I've fought off this piglet pretender, I'm a great guy, it cost you less than a million dollars – all sorted.'

His breathing is uneven. This is the first time in all our conversations, whether it was meeting personally or on the phone, that he has shown signs of nervousness.

'Steve, we'll agree that reasonable figure and for clarity I'll mention it and you agree it so we know what figure we're talking but we know what it is.'

Ackerman isn't the only one breathing heavily at this point. Me, I'm totally confused. I can't figure what Francis is at and just want him to come to the point.

'Of course we know what it is, Francis.' Ackerman's all affability but with just a soupçon of urgency in there, too. 'It's in the thousands.'

'Steve, it's been nice knowing you.'

No, it hasn't, Francis, why this extra crawling?

'Denise is here with me, she sends her regards.'

Like hell I send my regards.

'It's all over for us now and we wish you the very best.'

No, we don't wish him the very best. Or even the best.

'Yes, Francis. Now – what is the figure and what's your bank account number?'

Francis deals first with the second issue: the bank account number.

'It's Allied Irish Banks, 1 Lower Baggot Street. Are you taking this down?'

'Yeah.'

Francis chuckles softly, as if remembering the punch line to a joke.

'Steve?'

'Yeah?'

'Steve, I bet you're taping this. Disney tape everything, don't they?'

Ackerman laughs and says God no, Disney wouldn't tape conversations like this. Francis and I go nod, nod, nod madly at each other. Like children made certain that what is denied is in fact true.

'Steve, this is a settlement matter, can you confirm these words?'

'Sure, what do you want it to say?'

'Well, in Irish and English law we use the words "without prejudice".'

'Yeah, of course I'll confirm it's without prejudice.'

'Can we also use the American wording which is for settlement purposes only?'

Francis, I think, one of us – Ackerman or me – is going to kill you for not handing over your sword so it can be broken over Disney's knee. Get to the bloody point, would you?

With an audible effort at maintaining a patient calm, Ackerman confirms the conversation is for settlement purposes only, adding that he still doesn't have the settlement figure.

'Steve, you're not going to pay my costs?' Francis' voice is disbelieving, as if he's stupid and can't come to terms with that possibility.

'Francis. We don't want to go over that again.' Ackerman's not even pretending tolerance anymore. 'I'm not paying your costs. You are the author of your own misfortune.'

Francis does a big, sad, sigh. Like an animated character might do in a children's movie if he was very disappointed.

'Steve, I'll give you the reasonable figure now.'

24

Another sigh.

Francis Fitzpatrick, husband, father, lawyer and president of Piggley Pooh Inc., much as I love you, you're going to die by my hand in the middle of Boston. I'm going to murder you for bad acting and failure to surrender quickly when surrender is inevitable. The only issue is what weapon to use. Maybe that heavy glass ashtray.

'The figure is six times Disney's Pooh earnings worldwide,' Francis says in a defeatedly reasonable tone. 'That's $36bn,' he adds helpfully. 'Payable by Monday.'

Dead silence. Five seconds go by. Ten seconds. Thirty. A full minute. Silence, broken only by the noise of heavy breathing.

'Francis. You're joking?'

'Don't ever talk to me again,' Francis says icily. 'Get Eisner to phone me in future.'

He puts the phone down and that was it. I have my face covered in my hands, my shoulders shaking. Francis comes over to me and lifts my face, expecting tears. They're leaking out the corners of my eyes, but they come from laughter. The two of us cling to each other for about ten minutes, helpless with reckless laughter.

'You know what will happen now?' Francis eventually manages to ask. I shake my head.

'He has to go in to Eisner to say that he has the figure, the settlement figure. The board are all going to ask him what is it? And he's going to say "they're looking for $36bn"!'

It is surreal, the thought of Steve Ackerman, all contemptuous impatience a few minutes earlier, confidence coming out his very pores, now picking himself off the floor and going in to Disney's top man, Eisner, with the opposite of what Eisner's expecting. You don't tell Eisner bad news. This would be seriously bad news.

As our laughter dies, our fear reestablishes itself. If the

prospect of being hanged in the morning concentrates the mind wonderfully, let me tell you, the prospect of being crushed by the Disney corporation will do much the same. We've just thrown away half a million dollars, plus the deal with Mondo. Mondo won't bite if there's any possibility of litigation with that giant.

So we are on our own again. No money left. None at all. Return tickets and enough cash for a cab sit on the coffee table in the hotel room. We can make it to Logan Airport the following day and get on the flight home. We have more defiance than sense, I realise as I throw the coverlet of the bed back. Instead of concentrating on pulling a few bits from the wreckage, we've thumbed our noses and enjoyed doing it. The two of us stumble out of our clothes and into bed. We lie there, side by side, arms up, hands behind our heads, looking into the darkness, trying silently to convince our-selves that going down with all guns blazing is better than crawling away. Trying not to believe that maybe we've com-mitted the business version of 'suicide by cop', provoking our own killing by permanently enraging an international corporation that, in power terms, is as pervasive and potent as Microsoft or Merck.

'What's the beginning to that Dickens book?' Francis asks, his voice fuzzed with exhaustion.

It takes me a minute to understand the question.

'Which Dickens book?'

'*Tale of Two Cities*.'

It comes to me like the chorus of a song learned years earlier: '"It was the best of times, it was the worst of times …"'

'Yeah,' he said. 'That fits.'

The two of us say it out loud and laugh one final time before sleep overtakes us.

Chapter Two

A RIVER RAN THROUGH IT

I'm from a family of nine. Six sisters and two brothers. I'm the eldest. Home to the lot of us was a little village called Skryne, pronounced 'Screen'. Skryne is in County Meath, on the east coast of Ireland, about twenty-five miles north of Dublin and near the Hill of Tara, once the seat of the Irish high kings and now a major tourist attraction.

When I think of my childhood, it all seems to have taken place out of doors, in sunshine, in a magical place alive with the sounds of animals and the smell of fruits and flowers. Television was watched only when the weather was so bad that there was no alternative. We led an outdoor life, not just on our own farm, but on another farm, belonging to my grandfather, which was about a mile away. The farm belonging to my mother's family was about sixteen miles away. To a city person, one farm is much the same as another, but to the nine of us, each was crucially different from the others, so that between the three different places we had three different worlds.

Each was a crowded world with lots of siblings to play games with. But, as the eldest, I had an extra advantage. When my mother would go to visit her mother's farm, I'd get taken along. It was the same story when my father went to see his mother. As the first grandchild, I was specially welcome, hopelessly indulged, allowed to ear-wig on every conversation, hearing the family legends. Outside the house, I'd watch the animals and weave sagas in my head about what they did when I wasn't there to observe them.

Our home farm had a river running through it, and that was a big part of our childhood. Looking at it from an adult vantage point, it was little more than a stream, but to us children, it was a mighty river filled with endless possibilities. Every summer, when our cousins would come over to play, we'd go down to its banks, kick off our shoes and step into the icy water to collect pinkeens. Whole days would be spent down there. Although for most of its course through our land it was little more than a shallow trickle, at one point it deepened enough to allow us to jump in and get ourselves good and wet.

I remember one cousin of mine at a certain stage used to follow me around everywhere. We were great friends, but I was the boss, because it was my river. One summer day, I couldn't resist the urge to test out how far she would obey me.

'Go and jump in the river,' I ordered, as only a very small girl can order another very small girl.

Of course I was hoping she wouldn't do as instructed, but over she went and jumped in. I was trying to think up a good explanation for her being wet from head to foot when I realised the wetness was the least of my worries: on the way into the stream she had caught her foot and hurt herself. The whole saga became part of the mosaic of little anecdotes that add up to a family's history.

It was a lovely childhood – very happy. My mother was a brilliant homemaker, highly skilled at the tasks that create warmth and welcome in a house. It gave us children a wonderful unquestioning certainty: she was always there when we came in from school. We never came home to a cold house. That made such a difference. It freed all of us to enjoy childhood fully. We didn't feel worried about anything or burdened with anything.

From very early on, I was my own storyteller. My parents both worked very hard, and it was the details of what they were doing, especially with the animals, that I would find fascinating enough to spin into yarns. It helped that when dad came home he'd nearly always have a lollipop for me and, while I sucked it, I'd be listening to him talking about the machinery, the milking, the animals.

The animals were much more to us than pets or farm beasts. They were central to our lives and we loved them. We had sheep, we had horses and we had cattle. When the calves would arrive, we'd feed them. That's the great thing about growing up on a farm: each child has their work to do and they get a kick out of doing it well, but it never feels like work. My memories of childhood are bathed in sunshine. The weather seemed to be a lot sunnier than it is now.

I loved getting the picnics ready to bring to the men who were working down in the fields with my dad. Ham sandwiches, usually stuffed with my mother's home-baked ham, or salad sandwiches, based on home-grown lettuce, with its special taste. It wasn't just different, it was infinitely better than shop-bought lettuce. With salad cream. You grow out of the taste for salad cream, but as children, we loved it in the sandwiches. The smell of the sandwiches would make us starving and my mother would have to stress very strongly that none of us were to eat anything until permission was formally granted.

'All right, now, we'll have the sandwiches and tea,' my father would say, so casually, and we would restrain ourselves – with difficulty – from tearing apart the beautifully packaged food, which would have been carried to the field in a basket with a handle, everything tucked neatly into it and then a tea-cloth over it. Everything looked simple, although even the least complicated item, like the flask of tea, took time. Because teabags didn't exist at that time, the tea would be brewed in the teapot and then poured into a pre-warmed flask through a sieve. The sieve was to prevent tea-leaves landing in the flask and allowing the hot liquid to brew itself into dark-coloured tar. The sugar would be transferred from the big bag into a jar with a screw top, the milk – from our own cows – likewise.

Looking around me today, I see children clutching bottles of soft drinks from morning to night, but we never had Coke or Sprite. We were not imprinted with any of the brands so heavily marketed to children these days. Rather the reverse: we regarded anything bought in a shop as inferior to what was created in our farm, our garden or our kitchen.

My favourite task of all was haymaking in late summer. From us children's point of view, the best part was when the hay was baled. We could help stack the bales and convince ourselves that the men would have been lost without us. After an hour or so in the sunshine, we'd be really tired and we'd be dying for something to drink. Just at that point, Dad would always say: 'We'll sit on the bale and have some tea,' and out would come the cups and the sandwiches and it was great. They tasted better than any food ever tasted indoors.

But there were solitary times, too, when my lively imagination could come into play. That tended to happen when I found myself down in my grandmother's on my own. I'd go down to where the pigs were and watch the piglets scrambling and falling over each other and I'd think up stories about them. I remember looking in at the sty and thinking, about one of them, 'that's a real Piggley Pooh' and giggling at the sound of it. Then, every time I'd come down, the Piggley Pooh piglet was there and I'd be watching it grow and imagining the marvellous things he got up to when I wasn't there. He didn't get up to anything particularly marvellous when I was there, but children assume that magical things happen when they're not watching. That one little piglet, who never paid me that much attention, turned me into a storyteller. A storyteller, at that early stage, with an audience of one: me.

As I grew, I picked up – almost from the air – stories from Celtic mythology. Stories which were so rooted in my own kind of childhood that they felt familiar to me, even on first hearing. In the Celtic tradition, little streams and springs are endowed with mystical significance and are guarded by spirits. Even the pinkeens and other fish found in those streams represent spirits. In one of the most enduring legends, Fionn Mac Cumhaill works with the druid who guards the Salmon of Knowledge, and helps him when he cooks it. During the cooking, Fionn's thumb is scalded when he touches a blister on the skin of the fish, and the sum total of the world's knowledge seeps in through the wound. There-after, when he wants to know the answer to any question, all he has to do is suck his thumb. I remember, when I first heard the story of the Salmon of Knowledge, being quite convinced that I had caught his smaller, more modern brother among the pinkeens I brought home from the stream in a plastic pail.

It was a lot easier to dream dreams and tell myself stories at home than it was at school. I hated school. We went to a convent primary school. My mother was definitely ahead of her time in laying a huge emphasis on education. She had a really big family and was a committed homemaker. She knew the importance of education and didn't have a narrow view of what that was. She had us doing music, Irish dancing – everything that could stimulate our talents and build up our confidence.

It would have been a lot easier for my mother to send us into the local school, but she insisted that we start in the convent primary school in Navan because this ensured us a place in the attached secondary school later on. She had to drive us to school every day until we were teenagers, at which point we'd get buses. The commitment on her part was huge, when you think about the size of our family: seven sisters to be transported to a convent run by the Mercy Sisters and two brothers to St Finian's boys boarding school in Mullingar, which was run by the bishop of Meath. Parents these days complain about transporting their children to ballet, scouts and music classes, but this was at a time long before car-pooling. It was time-absorbing and demanding, but my mother made nothing of it, because she always saw education as the key to a worthwhile life.

I was far too young to appreciate her foresight when being kitted out with my schoolbag and marched into the convent every day, so I just hated the whole process. I felt trapped in primary school. Exceptional, in a negative sense. Relatively few country girls like me went to a convent primary school. Most of them tended to go to the local primary school. The only good thing about it was that we were musical as a family and, once they spotted this capacity, the sisters did encourage us to sing and play musical instruments.

Secondary school was a bit better. It was certainly a lot freer. The regimentation of every waking moment which had characterised primary schooling began to ease off as we grew old enough to take responsibility as individuals, rather than as members of a generic group.

Although I wasn't crazy about school at any stage, I knew it was essential to whatever I was going to do later on. That acceptance was matched by a fundamental optimism which I also trace back to my mother, who had – and still has – an enormous influence on me. Subconsciously, the quality of her thinking seeped into my own mindset. Far from dogmatic, she is the quietest woman you will meet. In fact, she is the sort of woman it's easy to take for granted. But behind her unassuming manner is a woman of enormous strength and dependability. When you grow up, as we did, never knowing what insecurity was, never threatened, never filled with dread, you are imbued with a buoyant optimism for the rest of your life.

She drew our attention to talents we wouldn't have known we had, so each of us felt special. She made me realise, for example, that I could read people. From her, I got a perception of myself as fairly astute and very much a 'do-er'. She made sure I was aware of my own potential, partly because she felt that I wasn't encouraged enough by the school, that I was overlooked there.

I passed my leaving certificate and got a few Cs but, although I had applied for entry to college, I just didn't see university as part of my life. I was never attracted to university life. The year I left school my grandmother was very ill, so my mom was constantly making trips to see her and look after her. With all that going on, it seemed to me that the best thing I could do was get a job. When I spotted an advertisement in the newspaper placed by a hotel in Dublin looking for a trainee receptionist, I decided to apply.

I didn't even know what a receptionist was, because as a family we had never needed to stay in a hotel, but the word 'trainee' attracted me, so I asked some of my friends what a hotel receptionist did. Their description made it sound fine so I was delighted when my application netted an invitation to come for an interview.

The interview was on a Saturday in Dun Laoghaire. Normally, each Saturday I went up to the Royal Academy of Music in Westland Row for music lessons, so I scheduled the interview to follow the music lesson. It sounded simple, except for the fact that I had no idea where Dun Laoghaire was. Getting lost was an inevitability, but at least I had company. For some reason I now can't remember, my younger sister Kay came with me. The two of us got on a number seven bus. So far, so good.

'Kay, we have to get off at Blackrock,' I told her, feeling totally in charge of the situation.

We duly got off at Blackrock only to discover we had to walk to Dun Laoghaire from there. I was convinced it would be a short walk. Logically, that's the way it had to be: we were on the seafront. The hotel was also on the seafront. Cheek by jowl, I figured. Shoulder to shoulder, I imagined. Side by side, even.

Nothing could have been further from the reality as Kay and I experienced it. The problem was that the seafront seemed to go on forever. We were walking faster and faster because I was now afraid of being late, the two of us exhausted and sticky and sharing flaky Tuc biscuits out of a packet so we were covered in crumbs.

Kay spotted the Marine Hotel.

'Denise, that must be it!' she said, delighted and relieved.

'That's not it,' I said, crossly. 'That's not the name of the hotel.'

She looked dismayed. The Marine was a big, impressive edifice. We walked on further and this much smaller hotel appeared, with the right name – the Hotel Pierre – out in front of it. In comparison with the grandeur of the Marine, it looked awful. Kay said nothing, but I knew what she thought. I said nothing, but what I thought matched what she thought.

'Never mind how it looks,' I told myself. 'You're going to do this interview. You're not going to have gone through all this for nothing.'

In the lobby of the hotel, I was met by a really tall, very well dressed woman who introduced herself as Miss Dermody. I instantly liked her, which improved my mood a bit. On the other hand, I was conscious that Kay was downstairs and related to her presence was a nagging question: how the hell are we going to get home? Because I was so distracted, I don't remember much of the interview but I did gel with Miss Dermody. I wasn't nervous. I was hot. I was sticky. I was surreptitiously brushing Tuc biscuit crumbs off myself. I had never done an interview before. I undoubtedly should have been nervous, but I had the courage of my ignorance.

Describing it as 'destiny' would be a bit heavy-handed for a job as a receptionist in a small hotel, but something said to me that I wanted to do this. This was the dream: to get up to Dublin and be independent. The odd thing is that I didn't know I had the dream until I was in the middle of the interview. It has happened throughout my life that I just seem to glide into situations. The consequences hit me afterwards and, be they good or bad, I deal with them.

In this case, the consequences were brilliant. Just a few days later, I got the phonecall offering me the job. It was a live-in position. 'All found.' The wages were small, but you were well looked after. So I was a trainee receptionist, living in the Pierre Hotel in Dun Laoghaire, getting my first pay packet.

It was only when I was on the job a few weeks that I realised the Pierre, at that time, wasn't a traditional hotel at all. The vast majority of the 'guests' were permanent. I was dealing every day with clients who lived there all of the time. It served as something like a retirement home for a particular clientele: elderly people with money who resided there and consumed all of their meals there.

Now and then, in addition, we would have guests who would come in from the boats. The hotel was located close to the port where the Stena ferry docked, so the odd passenger would meander up after they disembarked, looking for a room. They didn't know it was effectively a retirement home.

When my mom finally came up to see where her little

daughter was working, she was very upset. That kind of job, in that kind of hotel, was not what she wanted for me, at nineteen. But I was very happy. In fact, for me, it was arguably the perfect first job, the ideal introduction to being away from home and joining the workforce. I wasn't under pressure. I learned at my own pace. Some of what I learned would be useful to me later on. Some of it would be no use at all, based, as it was, on technology which, even then, was old-fashioned. For example, the hotel switchboard was one of those you see in old films, with hundreds of plug-in lines. Coming to terms with *that* was a major experience.

I stayed there for about a year and a half and then went next door to a real hotel run by two sisters and a brother, called the Carney Arms. All this time I was doing my music in the Royal Irish Academy. I studied both piano and violin as far as diploma level. Between the job, the music and trying to get home occasionally, it was a busy, happy time. I managed to get in a bit of social life, too. Indeed, it was when I was working at the Carney Arms that I met my first boyfriend.

I was less happy when, a couple of years later, I took a job in McDonalds in Rathmines. It wasn't a live-in job and commuting up and down to Rathmines from Skryne was tough going, forcing me to get up very early in the morning. Nor did I like McDonalds. I hated the mundaneness of it.

I had no idea what I wanted to do next. I just knew it had to be more interesting than serving hamburgers.

Chapter Three

MANAGEMENT – AND GIRLFRIENDS

One evening I was going to look at an apartment in Rath-mines, Dublin, when I met a girl with red hair, also named Denise, who planned to check out the same apartment. She was a lovely girl, from the country like me, living in Dublin while studying pharmacy. The two of us looked at the apart-ment. The two of us liked it. Except that the rent was too expensive for either of us. We came down the entrance steps, disconsolate, until it struck me that the apartment had two beds in it.

'You wouldn't like to share, would you?' I asked Denise.

'Well, actually I would,' she said. 'I need to. I *have* to. I'm a student.'

'So, do you want to share with me?' I asked.

She nodded, the two of us went back up the steps and we said we'd take it. We moved in and got on amazingly well, considering the impulsive way our relationship had begun.

A girl named Alison lived in the flat below and we were friends with her. I found her fascinating because she was kind of wild. Denise and I were reserved, compared with her, although of course we'd love to have been in the kind of company Alison socialised with.

On one particular evening, Alison happened to be coming in from work just as I arrived, and we talked in the hall. Towards the end of the conversation, she gave a big sigh: 'I've this bloody interview I'm supposed to go to,' she said. 'It's to get a position on a training course.'

'What's the course?'

'Quality management.'

'What's quality management?'

She gave me a quick and remarkably unenthusiastic rundown on what quality management was all about. It seemed to entail going into companies, particularly manufacturing companies, examining their procedures and improving them. Even though she didn't think much of it, to me, it sounded a lot more interesting than slinging hamburgers.

'Would you mind if I went to the interview, too?' I asked.

'Well, there's no "too",' she laughed. 'I've decided I'm not going. If you want to get on a quality management course, you're welcome to go to the interview instead of me!'

Which is precisely what I did – attended the interview in her stead. I have no idea what possessed me. I just liked what she said about it, even though she didn't like what she was talking about. I had no relevant experience. I didn't have a degree, if that was required. I had no notion that quality management was the new big thing. I went for the interview and got a place on the course, which was in the FÁS training centre in Loughlinstown.

Within a few weeks of the course, I began to make connections between what I was learning and some of what I had done before. Back when I had worked in McDonalds, they had all kinds of manuals applying to all the procedures – the procedures I found so mundane. That was quality control at one level. But what I was learning on the course was much more than that. It gave you the rationale behind such procedures and the practices they embodied.

Some of those attending didn't enjoy it. They got lost in the undergrowth, because they were getting too academic about it. I, on the other hand, found it easy and enthralling, because although I pay attention to detail I never get seduced by theory. I'm a doer. Quality management, I could see, was finding out, first of all, if something was working.

If it *was* working, you didn't interfere with it, but you did need to document it. Because you cannot assume that just because one particular team has worked out how to do something effectively and efficiently, the next team that comes along will do precisely the same thing.

Even though I had undertaken the interview on impulse without any career planning behind that impulse, I lucked out. The course just suited me. It suited my temperament and it suited my lack of worry about paperwork. It suited me because it was all about action and it was all about getting results at the end of the day. It was not a matter of opinion. It was about observation and documentation and doing things better. I liked it and it liked me – as I began to do it, and to find I could do it, my confidence and self-belief began to grow.

The course itself lasted for about twelve weeks. Then, newly-qualified, we had to go for job interviews and that's when I got my first break into the Smurfit corporation. I started working for a company called Irish Paper Sacks, in Walkinstown, as assistant manager, which impressed me to death because it was so different from anything I had done before.

Quality management was so new then that very few people, even in Smurfits, knew much about it. That was a great advantage to me. I couldn't be any worse than anyone else. I couldn't be compared with anyone else: nobody else had done the job before I did it. My mother had drummed into me that I'm a very quick learner, I'm good at reading people and I have an innate cop-on, so moving into a branch of a very big, very aggressive international corporation wasn't as hard as it might have been, even though I was without previous experience.

I moved quickly to try and get the plant the ISO9002 quality mark. Getting it would be a positive, not just on my

CV, but on the CV of the manager I worked for. I worked as if my life depended on it and, in due course, we got the ISO 9002 mark.

Having got into quality management by accident, I was now a proven expert in the field. Confident and eager for a new challenge, I decided I would prefer to be working for something with the Smurfit name on it. Although Smurfit owned Irish Paper Sacks, not many people realised it, and I felt it would be more prestigious to work for a company more clearly part of the Smurfit empire.

Somewhere, I got the nerve to go up against graduates and actually convince a senior personnel manager, the personnel director of Smurfits, to put me in a position of running a plant of 200 men. From nowhere – remember, up to then, my career had consisted of hotel reception jobs and a stint in McDonalds – I was one of the four senior managers reporting to a powerful chief executive in a major plant.

What made the job tough was that I was working in a male-dominated organisation. All the workers I dealt with as a quality manager were men. The few women in the plant were not on the factory floor. A scattering of female workers were to be found in areas like accounts, but in the nature of things, I had minimal contact with them. Nor, realistically, were they ever going to gel with me: I was locked in on the man's side of the operation and I was also part of the management. Unfortunately, as I was the only woman on the man's side, I wasn't quite part of that side, either.

I kept myself to myself. When I talked, I talked business, confiding no personal details to anybody, and never socialising with co-workers. When, these days, I hear myself describe those years, it sounds bleak. It wasn't.

I had fun and companionship and trust in plenty. I had them from my friends and my family. Deciding not to pursue them at work meant that, in an aggressively male corporate culture, I was able to be a loner and be seen to be a tough loner. I could give as good as I got from the guys on the factory floor.

Once the novelty of a woman working among them and observing the processes of their jobs wore off, the guys realised that I wasn't setting out to be either impressive or aggressive. I didn't flirt, either. All I wanted was the work done in a particular way and, when the operatives realised that what I was trying to spread were the methods and standards the best guys used, they responded warmly and positively to what I was doing.

I went in with great confidence that I could capture the best of the procedures they had in place and perhaps improve them, and I did. This gave me a reputation in a new area, an area that was beginning to be seen as important, as making a contribution to the bottom line.

Next step up the Smurfit ladder meant taking on a consultancy in Smurfit Corrugated Cases in Cork. Accepting it – which I did – meant moving everything I owned 250 kilometres to Cork. That, as it turned out, was the easy bit.

It was a tough beginning in a new location. As the driver of quality, I was seen as a threat to the men working there because I'd have to go into each department and see where the shortfalls were. But when I'd come up with methods of tightening up the process so it would withstand the examination of the outside quality people – who had the power to accredit us with our quality mark – the threat receded.

I could have been the punitive police officer, coming in to find them doing things wrong. But Smurfit obviously was a successful company. It didn't need to be changed, it just needed to be documented and tightened up. On arrival to each plant, I was not setting out to find them doing something wrong. I was setting out to discover simply what they were actually doing. Most of the time, what they were doing was right, so all that was missing was a method of documenting that and guaranteeing it for the future.

I then had to combat the feeling that 'OK, now the quality thing is done'. Because, of course, 'the quality thing' is never done. The first step may be the winning of accreditation, but after that must come continuous improvement so that, even when you get the mark, you are committed to making it even better.

Those tough early months were at least made easier by the fact that being based in Cork didn't affect my family or social life. Smurfits appreciated that I had relocated at relatively short notice and, as a result, when I'd want to go up to Dublin, they'd pay my train fare or give me a car. A certain amount of flexibility was built into their expectations anyway, because I was working on a consultancy basis. This meant that when I went to Dublin or Meath for the weekend, I didn't have to get back to the Cork plant first thing Monday morning.

I was dictating my life: my working life and my social life. I hadn't had a serious relationship since my first one, back when I was working in the Carney Arms hotel, but I loved going out socialising with my friends. I had a cousin, Anne Bannon, who worked in the hotel business in Drogheda, and I used to go over there to visit. We were very giddy. Work was serious. Social life was not.

While I was working in Cork, I got romantically involved with one of the graduates working for me. His dad was vice president of Smurfits in America. He was my first really serious boyfriend and I still feel warmly towards him. It never came to anything between us because of a confluence of circumstances. He went back to the US to do his master's but he only did it because he thought I wanted him to do it. I thought I did want him to get it because it would be good for him. But I may have thought he wanted to do it more than he actually did and, as a result, I was consciously not standing in the way of his academic career.

Whatever the reasons, the fact is that we had a pleasant relationship that ended without damage to anybody. It's not always easy to achieve that when both parties are working in the same company, and it's even less easy to achieve it when the woman is the boss, as I was.

One of the problems at the time was that any successful woman in any area of a large company like Smurfits was assumed to be dying to meet any other successful woman within the company. Sandra, a successful saleswoman within Smurfits, made an appointment to see me, pushed by male colleagues convinced that we'd love each other on sight. We didn't. Mainly because I was all business.

'You know, my time is precious,' I said briskly, with a 'tell me what you want and get out' expression on me.

Sandra had been told 'you two girls will love each other on sight, and you should probably share an office ...' She had all the characteristics that made her a great salesperson. I had all the characteristics that made me a good manager. The result was initial disaster. She went right back to her boss in a rage: 'I'm not sharing with *that* bitch!'

But that – fortunately – wasn't the end of it. Not long afterwards, the two of us encountered each other again, socially. Sandra realised that, although it takes me a little while to warm up, I warm up well. In no time at all, we not only found ourselves sharing an office, but decided to rent an apartment together and were bosom pals. Enduring pals. Sandra Sheridan is still the bubbly effervescent person I roomed with in Cork. She is the mother of two boys and continues to work in sales.

Back then, as young independent women with our own sense of style and *joie de vivre* we really had a carefree enjoyable time in Cork. We loved working out in the local gym –

Sandra is very disciplined about fitness and diet – and then heading off to one of the pubs where most young people met and socialised.

Strong friendships with women are central to my life. I see them as much more than social. You learn from good friends. I certainly learned from Sandra. I would watch her with delight. She was amazing. She has a bubbling personality, which is why she is a good saleswoman. We mightn't have started off as best friends, but once I got to know her, I really admired her. Watching her, I suspect, improved my own social skills, too. I could see that she was well able to fit in with the men in this very male-dominated business and had everyone liking her at the same time. She was able to do her job without being as boundary-conscious as I was. So I began to think about just how much I needed to be as coolly detached as I thought I needed to be, and I probably became a little more equable, a little more fun to work with. She softened me.

The apartment we shared had enough room for a third person, so the two of us got launched on a project: to interview guys who might make acceptable flat-sharers. We used important criteria such as he had to be goodlooking but not the kind of guy either of us would fancy. The flatmate we picked was Ray Lacy, who met both specs and, in addition, was from Cork and so would have an inside track on local social life. He had competition. One guy ran him close, but had long hair which neither of us really liked. So we opted for Ray.

Not only was he a great flatmate but he operated on such a tight routine that we really didn't need a clock. If it was 7.50 in the morning, Ray would be up and in the shower …

Another girl who turned out to be a lifelong friend was Miriam, who was introduced to us by her brother, Patrick, after we met him in the Wilton Pub and Restaurant. Miriam shared a room with me in Cork and we had many happy times together as we forged a deep and lasting friendship. I also met another lifelong friend, Arlene, and the three of us became known as the MAD team for our exploits in socialising. Miriam now has her own interior design business in Dun Laoghaire called Minnie Peters. Arlene is also a successful interior designer with her own company, Velvet. Sandra is managing director of Auto Trader. My cousin, Anne, who I probably see most these days, has two Remax auctioneering businesses in Meath.

Each of us was a focused, ambitious businesswoman. Each of us had a great social life. But at the same time, we were learning what was important – what was really important – about each other. Sandra, for example, never does emotional blackmail. She never got angry with me, never sulked, never fought. I can't imagine being friends with someone who fights or goes cold. If I have a disagreement with someone, I want to sit down, thrash it out and move on without any trailing unpleasantness. Each of my women friends, although they're unique and quite different from each other, are warm strong people. We could – and did – live in each other's pockets and then not see each other for a while, yet pick up where we left off.

At that time, European legislation was coming in which dealt with women in the workforce. This legislation was making it very clear to employers that the old rationales as to why women did not get promoted to management would not be acceptable in the future. Women in the workplace were equal citizens. They were to be recruited on the same basis as men, as opposed to being asked who was going to mind their children if the children got sick, or even, as sometimes happened, being asked when they were getting married or planning to have children. They were to be paid the same. And they were to be promoted on merit, just as men were.

Most big companies at the time went through a kind of forced examination of conscience. Not just big commercial firms, but public sector bodies and government departments, too. At that time, for instance, there had never been a woman appointed as a secretary (or, as they're now titled, director-general) of a government department. A woman could be highly qualified, could spend her entire working life in a department, could be provably competent, yet never be promoted beyond a predictable level.

Smurfits certainly addressed the issue, circulating a memo throughout all plants to the effect that the company would have to employ more women at all levels. The notices going up on noticeboards in Smurfit plants – in common with plants belonging to most industrial sectors around that date – changed so that a gender preference was neither expressed nor hinted at. Interview patterns changed too. In a sense, a kind of affirmative action pattern happened within Smurfit: during a period after the EU legislation came in, the corporation concentrated, not just on staying within the law, but perhaps on balancing the odds for women a little. Given the overwhelmingly male culture I and other women of my time had encountered, this was probably a good thing.

Around this time, Smurfits bought UK Corrugated in England and, in due course, as is standard throughout the organisation, they started posting notices throughout the Irish Smurfit plants of jobs to be filled in England. I just started applying for posts that looked promising. I remember Dermot Killen coming in to my office.

'Do you really want to go over to England?' he asked.

'Well, if it means that I move up into a senior position and can later move back to Ireland at that level, then yes, why not?' I asked.

He shrugged.

'It's a huge commitment,' he pointed out.

My turn to shrug. From the moment I had started working, I had tended to work in locations far from my home and to uproot after a period of time – precisely the period of time most people use to set down roots and create social networks – and move on to something more challenging in a quite different location. Dermot was left in no doubt that I could handle that kind of commitment, and so wasn't surprised when another quality management position came up in Britain and I applied for it.

They flew me over for an interview at a plant in West Auckland with the boss, Ray Newell.

The offices were fabulous. Mine in particular. It may sound a bit previous to say 'mine' but that's the way it felt, even on that first, supposedly tentative, visit. I was there to let them see me and interrogate me, and I was going through that process but *my* office was calling to me so loudly, it drowned out half of what was going on. Mine was a huge office with big glass windows and black furniture.

'This is unbelievable,' I thought. 'I want it. I want it now.'

And I convinced Ray Newell to give the job – and the office – to me, right there and then.

It wasn't easy, I found out later. Ray was frankly afraid of taking on a woman, particularly an Irishwoman. With some reason. 'This is mining country,' he told me afterwards. 'The people who work at this plant are mining stock, and it's a tough breed. Plus, you're talking about people who have been here for twenty or thirty years and here was this Irish girl in her early twenties coming in to change their work habits.'

Never mind the legislation that says you have to employ more women in management. It still takes courage and faith to appoint a female to quality management in that kind of situation. Ray fished around a bit and found that I was seen as resilient and was always tough and detached. But the scale of the job was going to be huge – totally different to what I had done in Ireland. This was total responsibility and being a senior manager and having to present and run the plant with the chief executive. Although he went through the interviews with other (male) candidates, he decided to take the risk and offer the position to me.

I remember getting the contract. Where it dealt with salary, it said: £35,000 sterling. That was a lot of money at that time. Remember, the year was 1993. In that year, the average wage in Ireland was £7,000. I remember going to the Chinese restaurant in Navan with three girls I'd met in Cork who've been an important part of my life every since. Before the food was served, I took out the contract and showed it to my friends.

'Omigod,' they said. '*Omigod.*'

There were hugs and congratulations all round, with all of us getting in the way of the arriving waiter. The girls were glad for me. Because they were my friends. Because it was a great breakthrough job for any woman at that time. And because they knew that I'd just come through a difficult patch in my emotional life in that my second boyfriend and I had gone our separate ways.

Chapter Four

MEETING A MAN ON THE FOURTH OF JULY

If you could separate your love affairs from your career, life would be a lot easier to manage. At this particular juncture in my own career, I was heading for the office of my dreams in Britain, but I was also standing in the wreckage of a romantic relationship.

The conclusion of my relationship with the American boyfriend had been painless enough on all sides. It was what happened afterwards that complicated my life. When offered this new job, I had another guy. Except that this man was very much not just 'another guy'. I was convinced, for the first time in my life, that I was in love. This new man and I had a lot in common, starting with a shared background in farming.

Of course, farming is not the best business to be in when it comes to socialising. Every now and then, some seasonal aspect of his work would interfere with some big date. The Galway races has always been a big part of my year. I'm mad about horses, for starters, and the Galway race-meeting, as anyone interested in horse racing will tell you, is one of the best. It happens in high summer and the organisers tend to be incredibly lucky when it comes to weather. My sense of the races is of me and my girlfriends dressed to the nines in light floaty summer dresses, sometimes with great hats, washed in sunshine and enjoying the fantastic informal buzz of the three days.

The year I began to get really fond of this other guy, I planned, as always, to go to the Galway races with my friends. I went, but for the first time in my life did so in two minds.

I actually wanted to get back because my boyfriend couldn't be there. He was harvesting his potatoes or whatever his crop was. He was delighted that I was going, but I wasn't. Myself and this group of pals had travelled to the west: three girlfriends I'd met in Cork, together with Anne, my cousin, and a bunch of her friends, all genuinely interested in horses. It was wonderful, but I was distracted. Distracted, first of all, because my farmer boyfriend wasn't there. But there was another complication. On 4 July, exactly three weeks before Galway, I had met this lawyer named Francis Fitzpatrick. Although that first meeting wasn't exactly romantic.

We met in O'Dwyers pub in Lower Mount Street at a Fourth of July party in 1993, mainly frequented by nurses from Holles Street Maternity Hospital. The night of the party, Francis was at the bar with a male friend of his, Francis Rowan. I was there with my cousin, Anne Bannon. It was the other Francis who started the conversation, which is unusual, because, as I was to find out, in any group, it's usually Francis Fitzpatrick who makes the first conversational move, essentially because he has no social fears whatsoever.

You could put him down in the middle of a sumo wrestling contest and he'd strike up a conversation with any of those fat guys with the nappies on them. Doesn't matter that they don't know each other. Doesn't matter that these might be the most acclaimed sumo wrestlers in the world. Doesn't matter that they may have no interest in a lawyer named Fitzpatrick. Francis goes into every social situation convinced that he's going to like the people he meets and they're going to like him. The annoying thing is how often that conviction plays out in reality.

Francis Rowan started to talk to Anne at a point in the party when I had gone off to the ladies' room. Francis Fitzpatrick got dragged into the conversation and sat down in the handiest seat – mine.

I came back from the ladies, and there was this guy planted in my chair, all chat and confidence and charm. I stood in front of him. 'That's my seat,' I said.

I wasn't rude about it, but I did want to sit down. He seemed delighted to give it back to me. A few civil words passed between us but I didn't feel he was interested in me, and I wasn't that interested in him. (Later, I found out that he'd recently broken up with his girlfriend and was just out to have a good time that night: a few drinks with the lads and a really good old chat.)

For some odd reason, Francis decided to put on an accent and pretend he was an American in Dublin that night for an American football game due to happen in Lansdowne Road. He was going, full throttle, on this impersonation, when I interrupted.

'You're no more American than I am,' I said.

'OK,' he said, and shrugged.

It should have been an end-of-story moment, but in fact it was probably the first time we really registered each other. He noticed, he claims, that I had 'these most wonderful piercing blue eyes'. I liked the way he abandoned the phoney accent and picked up talking normally. He didn't care about being found out.

What followed on from that was that we asked the two guys their names.

'I'm Francis and he's Francis.'

Yeah, right, I thought, but decided to play along just a little more.

'What do you do?'

They both said they were solicitors. Myself and Anne at this point, without even a mutual glance, decided the two of them were just playing silly games. I really thought that they were messing at that stage. Saying they were both Francis and both solicitors clearly couldn't be the truth and wasn't very imaginative. 'Right, ok, if you want to play it like that,' I said.

When myself and Anne got ready to leave, they asked us were we going down to a nightclub called Howl at the Moon.

'No, we're not,' I said. 'We think we'll go down to the Burlington.'

Which we did and got into a good corner in the VIP section, because I knew one of the PR managers there. That was pretty standard for the two of us. Even when we would go to the races, we wouldn't have badges but we would just walk by the stewards – they wouldn't stop us. Or in any nightclub with one of those fenced-off inner circle areas: we'd just go in. I don't know where we got the effrontery from but we'd just do it. It was all fun, all part of a great time in our lives.

On this particular night, the two 'Francises' followed us down to the Burlington. They maintain, to this day, that it was a coincidence, that they didn't follow us down, but they've never convinced Anne and me. They followed us. Francis Fitzpatrick tried to get in to the inner circle by passing himself as one of the Fitzpatricks who own hotels, but the bouncers didn't buy it and left the two of them out with the plebs, while Anne and I were up with the movers and shakers.

The simplest thing to do was forget about him and concentrate on enjoying my night, just as the simplest thing for him to do was concentrate on the people around him in the 'coach class' of the nightclub. Neither of us did the simple thing. I found a series of reasons to go out of the VIP area to check how he was doing because, of course, he couldn't get into where I was. Anne always asked afterwards why I went out to him that night and I have never had a good answer for her. I just did it.

The payoff for my social Red Cross act wasn't great.

Whenever I'd go out – and I went out more than once, he'd be talking to some girl. I don't know whether he engineered it or it just happened. So I'd arrive out and he would be playing it cool.

'If you want to come out, come out of the VIPs and be with the commoners for once,' he'd say, and turn back to the girl he was chatting up. On the one hand he was giving me a victory look that said 'it's not a good idea to leave me out here, I'll always find someone else,' but on the other hand, he always broke off the conversation he was in to talk to me or include me in it. It was all playful and enjoyable. Or so I thought, until I offered him a lift home and got a fast refusal – he already had a lift home.

A few weeks later, he rang me. I spent the first couple of minutes of the telephone call trying to remember if I'd given him my number. (He told me later that although he'd decided I was inconsiderate to stay up in the VIP section, he'd still been interested enough to make sure he had a point of contact.) I didn't have to try to remember *him*. He suggested he might take a trip south to see me in Cork. A couple of weeks after that visit, I came up to Dublin and stayed over in Rathgar with him because we were going out to a nightclub and staying out late. I began to like him a lot, and he me. He guessed that I was dating someone else at the time.

'My experience of girls is: "this is an attractive girl, she ain't on her own so don't ask too many questions and enjoy yourself and get on with it",' is how he sums up his attitude at the time. It wasn't far from my own mindset.

It all seemed casual and easygoing, but in fact, my future was being laid out for me. A bunch of factors were coming together that would change several lives. Factor 1 was being offered the job in Smurfits UK with the big office. Factor 2 was a green Citroen Diane I bought from my sister who was in London and brought it over to me on the ferry. This was before the NCT test, when you took your chances with cars, even ones like this where the wiring was all exposed. It could have blown up at anytime. It chose to blow up in Cork and burst into flames just before I was due to go to England.

Put those two factors together and what you get is me with a serious need of a car to get my property to my new home in England. Factor 3 was the Merc I tried to hire for that purpose.

'Where in England can I leave this car back?' I asked as I was leaving the hire place. Faces fell all around.

'Oh, you're bringing the car to England?'

'Yes,' I said, restraining myself from adding 'since when has England become Outer Mongolia?'

'We can't insure you in England.'

'Now you tell me!'

I was car-less again. The Merc was full of my stuff but I couldn't drive it to where I needed to go. So I rang my farmer boyfriend. 'Can you help me, please?' I asked. 'Will you drive my stuff over to England with me?'

The short answer was no. The long answer was that he couldn't do it because he was really busy on the farm at that time of the year, which I must have known really.

'Well, how the hell am I going to get my stuff over there?' I asked him, knowing well that it made him feel awful and that there was nothing he could do about it.

When I rang off, I convinced myself that I had no option, at this stage, other than to telephone Francis Fitzpatrick who I knew had a car – an Alpha Romeo – of which he was very proud. In fact, he was so proud of it that, looking back, I realise that in asking him to transport luggage in it, I was insulting his beloved vehicle just a bit. But I never thought about that, any more than I considered the possibility that he would refuse the request. The fact that he operated his law practice as a sole practitioner and that absence from his desk meant absence of income didn't even strike me. I was completely focused on a useless Merc packed to the gills with my clothes, books, records and general paraphernalia. It was time for Plan B, and I was offering Francis a chance to star in Plan B.

His response was immediate. Of course he would drop everything and bring my property to England in his luxury car. He got directions from me and told me he'd be with me within half an hour. When he arrived, we loaded all the things out of the Merc into his Alpha. At that point, he followed me into the car rental offices where I handed back the keys. Disgusted with the guys there because they had put me to such bother and wasted so much of my time, as I handed back the keys, I let them have it. Francis stood there, silent. It wasn't until many months later he told me how appalled he was by me dressing down the hire company staff. Francis – as this book makes very clear – will fight to the death for what he believes in, but would never get shirty over being inconvenienced by a bureaucratic mix-up.

Because I was still enraged with the rental company and he was bothered by my showing it so bluntly, we drove to the ferryport in almost total silence, sunk in our own thoughts. At the port, Francis asked me if I had a passport. I didn't. Eventually, I found my driver's licence. Meanwhile, he was flicking through all his documentation. I was mesmerised. Here I was with a lousy driver's licence to identify myself, and this man, in contrast, had about twelve different forms for himself.

'Francis,' I said, beginning to laugh, 'it's me who's moving!'

I just couldn't believe that this guy could be so organised and he couldn't believe that I was just going over with a licence. He just couldn't believe it. He was shocked by it. I just thought this was so funny, I had difficulty getting out of the car, and over the next few hours, every time I thought about it, I would laugh out loud all over again.

We disembarked and began the drive to West Auckland. Just outside Leeds, Francis filled the car with petrol and had gone in to pay for it when it suddenly dawned on me that I had nowhere for him to stay. I hadn't thought it through. I had sort of expected him to simply turn back, after he'd unloaded me and my goods, and go back to Ireland.

'Oh my God, Francis,' I said. 'Where are you going to stay? I've nowhere for you to stay.'

He nearly crashed the car. He could not believe what I had done: 'You didn't book me a room in the hotel?'

'No, I didn't think, I suppose I thought you'd turn and go back.'

At this point, he went over a bollard in his good car.

'We'll get to a phonebox and I'll ring and I'll get you in,' I said, trying to mollify him and distract him from the possibility of stopping the car to examine if the bollard had done it any damage.

This was night time, when it was difficult to get a hotel room, but I let on to be more confident than I was, and fortunately they had one. 'Fortunately' because I was beginning to realise how much I fancied this man. I liked him a lot, now that I was starting to really get to know him – and there's no way as good for getting to know someone as sharing a long car and sea journey with them.

I liked that he knew everything. I liked that I could respect his opinion because an awful lot of men I met just wouldn't have the confidence to have and support opinions on anything but their direct area of work. I liked a man who would make decisions. He was great at organising things. He was intellectually clever, but didn't have the helplessness I associated with academics. I hated helpless men who could not do anything. Plus, he was interesting.

Inevitably, I found myself comparing him with my farmer boyfriend. It was unfair to the farmer to think of him as having let me down, but I did think of him as having let me down. Certainly, when I compared his response to the reaction of another self-employed man – Francis – who had dropped everything at a moment's notice, even though he didn't know me half as well, Francis came out of the comparison looking very good indeed. He looked even better in the following week, because he ended up closing his office for ten days and stayed to help me. He got my car organised and he brought all my stuff into work.

That was the start of Francis and me. That was the point when I knew I loved him. During the week he stayed in England with me, I never got lonely. But I felt very lonely and I felt something was missing when he was going. I didn't want him to go, even though I knew he had to. I knew he felt the same because, before he left, he secretly planted little figurines all over my home with little messages under them. It was like a treasure hunt: each message would tell me to look somewhere else and when I'd look there, there'd be another message – so, every night for the first few after he left, there was something somewhere in the house to ease my loneliness.

Little frogs and rabbits peeped out at me from the oddest angles, with a lovely message under each. Nobody had ever done anything like that for me before. It showed me he was obviously feeling something too. We never really discussed it but I definitely knew I was getting unsettled. Francis was equally unsettled, he says today: 'When I went over there and spent the week, we got very close. I started to like this girl a lot and thought she was funny and cute. She made me laugh. She laughed at my jokes, which made me feel important, special, interesting. She was interested in me. We became quite close quite quickly.'

As I started in the new job, I began to go over and visit

Francis in Dublin. We started semi-officially going out together then. He stopped seeing other girls and I ended it
with my farmer. What quickly became a real problem was
that the only airline that flew to Newcastle was Aer Lingus
and, because they had a monopoly on the route, they were
charging £300 for a return ticket. Now this was quite a while
back, when the Irish punt was worth something. £300 in
those days – Francis wouldn't have earned that in a week. So
he began to say to himself: 'You must really like this girl if
you're prepared to spend this type of money visiting her.'

It was fun at the beginning but as time went on, it got
impractical for me to be going over there and him coming
over to me. It was July when we first met. By October, we
were getting very close. By November or December we were
extremely close and Francis proposed on 28 December 1993,
when we had known each other less than six months.

Francis, at thirty-three, was beginning to envy friends of
his who had settled down, particularly the ones with children. His sister had two or three kids at this stage and he just
loved those kids. He was particularly close to his niece, Freya,
who's also his godchild. On the one hand, he was having a
great life. He could have looked at the relationship with me
as an update on his earlier relationship with his girlfriend in
Canada. After all, not being tied down has its own rewards.
But by Christmas that year, it was all falling into place for
him. He wanted me. He wanted marriage. He wanted children. Typically Francis, he remembers it as full of romantic
significance – but as a marketing opportunity as well: 'My
experience of relationships was that they can go on forever
or they can have a meaning. I wanted this to have a meaning. So I saw the walk in Bushy Park as an opportunity to
close the deal …'

I was getting ready to fly back to Newcastle after the
Christmas holidays. Now, at some earlier stage we had talked

idly about where each of us would like to go on our honeymoon. The honeymoon conversation happened long before it was relevant to us, but I remember suggesting Hong Kong, where he had lived as a child, would be a great place to go. So, post-Christmas, the two of us were walking around Bushy Park when Francis said in a heavily casual tone, 'So will we go to Hong Kong?'

That was his 'proposal'.

'You're not getting away with that,' I said. 'You have to do the whole lot of a proper proposal.'

'You're not going to make me go down on one knee?' he asked.

'I am,' I said.

So that's what happened. In Bushy Park. On a path. Francis went down on one knee and said 'Will you marry me?'

'Of course,' was my reply. I had no second thoughts. When he asked me I knew it was the right thing to do. The way he tells it, he was just as certain.

'I felt you were someone I'd like to spend the rest of my life with,' is how he puts it.

It helped that when he drove me over to Newcastle, he realised that I was not only a senior executive, but one of five people running a plant of 200 workers.

'Any time I'd go over I'd see you at work. I'd get a kick out of someone so small ordering these massive guys around. I just thought you had tremendous verve and energy and I'm thinking, "my god this girl is a dynamo – she is so driven. She's a tremendous person." I felt that you could accomplish anything. I was very impressed by you.'

It's unbelievable that, after such a short space of time, both of us could be so sure. The giveaway for each of us was probably the fact that we began to find it so hard to part from each other every time he came over to see me. These were huge feelings for both of us. Huge feelings. Huge commitment – and no worries about it. There was no worry. Partly because we had discovered, early on, that each of us had a strong religious faith. That was one of the things that attracted me way back at the Galway races. Because he said to me 'I'll pick you up after mass' and I knew a lot of people didn't go to mass when they went to Galway races.

I always went to mass because I've always seen Sunday as sacred. So, when he said that to me, completely unselfconsciously, I thought to myself, 'that's nice'. Then we would say the rosary when we started dating. We always said the rosary at home and when we'd go on car journeys. One day, when Francis and I were out on a date, going somewhere that required a sizeable drive, it seemed natural to me to suggest the continuation of what I'd always done in my own family.

'Will we say the rosary?' I asked.

He was surprised, but not taken aback.

'Yeah, why not?' was his reaction.

I gave out the rosary, he responded and in that fifteen minutes, we discovered we had something else in common: our religious faith. The great thing about the discovery was how simple it was. Neither of us felt at risk that the other would be facetious about it. Francis is sometimes funny about his faith, but never facetious.

Even before Francis proposed to me in Bushy Park, I had become totally unsettled in Newcastle. I wanted to come home. Then came the proposal, which happened on the night before I was due to go back to my job.

'Fran,' I said. 'The only problem is, I can't go back to Newcastle.'

I meant (I know now) that I didn't want to go back to that job and that location at all. Francis thought the issue was more immediate. He wanted me to go back to Newcastle without telling my parents about our engagement.

'I can't do that,' I told him. 'I just can't. I just can't believe this has happened to me. Nobody's married in my family. My sisters have been doing longer lines than you and me.'

'All the more reason for you to leave it a bit. There's no real realisation in your family as to how close we are.'

That was true. Not all of my siblings had even met Francis at that point. My parents had met him once or twice, but I was shy about him. I don't know why. I just didn't tell anybody before he proposed that I was falling in love with him. Plus, I was in England and when I was meeting him in Newcastle on his visits there, my friends and family weren't around to notice what was happening.

'No,' I said, suddenly digging in my heels. 'We're going to do this properly.'

'How d'you mean, properly?'

'You have to ask my father.'

'I hardly *know* your father!'

'Yes, but you love horses and that's the one thing that my father loves, horses.'

Francis worked hard at getting his head around this as we left Bushy Park. He had no choice. My father was always the most important man in my life up to the time I met Francis, because he was just a rock. He's always there and consistent – he never changed.

Francis came into the house that day, and my mother was baking – flour everywhere and her apron on, oblivious to the impending news of her daughter's wedding plans, as was my dad. I was trying to get an opportunity for Francis and my father to get together but my brother and sister were there and it was difficult to disentangle him. It was back to the common love of horses, I figured.

'Dad, Francis loves horses,' I said. 'Would you go down and show him your horse, *Persian Life?*'

Dad was delighted. But of course Eimear and Jimmy – my brother and sister – said 'can we come too?' Francis was very nervous. I was full of expectation. I was dying to tell my mother but I wanted confirmation from Francis, so when he came back in, I was all eagerness until the slight shake of his head sent the message that he hadn't done the deed. Time was ticking on. I had to get to the airport. I was trying to work out what I should do next.

'Will you show Francis the good rooms?' I said to my father, who looked at me as if I'd lost it.

'Francis doesn't want to see the rooms,' he pointed out, accurately, knowing that whereas a girlfriend might be interested, it was different if it was a man.

'He does,' I said through gritted teeth. 'He really does. Don't you, Francis?'

'Oh, yes,' Francis said. 'The rooms – oh, yes.'

My father got up again, totally mystified that a sensible big fella like Francis who's into horses would want to look at newly-decorated rooms, but prepared to go along with it if it made me happy, and off the two of them went, leaving me with Mom, still baking, still oblivious to everything. I slid over beside her.

'Mammy, he's askin',' I said. 'He's askin' daddy.'

'Asking him what?' my mother asked, puzzled.

'He's askin' – we're going to get married,' I said.

'Oh my God,' she gasped and started cleaning the flour off her hands. She was just totally mesmerised because this was the first, this was the start of the marriages of her children. Then Francis comes down, red-faced and my dad with him, all delighted, having told Francis that himself and my mother would be very glad for the two of us. It was lovely. And then I said to Francis – poor Francis – 'Francis do you want to go out and drive around in the car and I'll be out in a minute.'

Because I wanted to be with my family before I headed off to the airport. To hold and be held. To laugh and to weep. God love Francis, he was driving around and around while all this family stuff was going on. Eventually, I tore myself away from them with far too little time left to get me to the airport and went back to England.

It was the biggest moment in my life, there in our family kitchen. It was all warmth and happiness and the confidence that this was the man and that we were right for each other. The only cloud on the horizon was my job. What was I going to do? We decided to get married in October 1994. I knew Smurfits would not look on this positively. They had trusted me with a senior position and would take a dim view of me marrying so quickly.

Because I knew the reaction would be negative, I just avoided facing up to it. Two months passed without my saying anything about Francis to anybody in Newcastle. Two months of planning and postponing, of phonecalls and secret wedding plans.

Chapter Five

FROM INDIAN SUMMER TO CHILLY BOARDING SCHOOL

Francis was born in Bombay in India, in 1960. So, where my earliest memories are all about a farm in Meath, with its cows and pigs and chickens, his are all about India and about the beautiful three-acre garden in Madras where he and the other Fitzpatrick children used to play. It was so beautiful, a couple of films were shot in it.

The family, at that time, had a very privileged lifestyle. One of the reasons for that was that his father was a banker. Another was that, although Britain had ceded India's independence back in 1948, not a lot had changed. The professional classes – particularly Irish and British expatriates – could live extraordinarily well on salaries which would have been respectable, but no more than that, back in their countries of origin. Francis' family had servants and even drivers. Not only was his first language not Irish, it wasn't even English: he and his brother spoke a dialect of Hindi to each other rather than English when they were babies because that was the language their nanny spoke. Oh, and lest you should think they had to share a nanny, that wasn't the case. Each of the little boys had their own nanny. The nannies conversed in Hindi and so the two little boys did, too.

In 1964, the family moved from India to Hong Kong, where his dad worked for the Mercantile Bank, a subsidiary of the Hong Kong and Shanghai Bank. For two years, Francis and his brother, Patrick (older by one year), attended school there. They may have found fluency in Hindi easy, but Mandarin – which was on the curriculum in Hong Kong

– was a very different story. Mention lessons in Mandarin to Francis and he automatically shakes his head. He found it impossible to learn back then and, when he re-visited it more recently, didn't get much further with it.

Difficulties in his Hong Kong school with Mandarin, however, were nothing compared to the difficulties he was to face in the next couple of years. At that time, families working in locations like Hong Kong believed that sending their children home to boarding school in Ireland was considered the best educational option. So that's what happened. The two brothers, Patrick, who was seven, and Francis, who was just six, were sent to a school called Killashee outside Naas in County Kildare. Killashee is now a five-star luxury hotel but it was spartan when the two little boys arrived there. The let-down, as they arrived, was stomach-churning.

'It had been sold to us as an exciting place where little boys played soccer and rugby,' Francis remembers. 'My parents gave the impression that it was such a wonderful place, you'd never want to come home after it. My mother flew with my brother, Patrick, myself and my sister, Mary, from Hong Kong to Dublin. I will never, ever forget the cold in Heathrow and Dublin airports – snow – we were coming from a sunny climate. We stayed in the Four Courts Hotel that night and I never heard wind rattle as I heard that night. We were terrified and very glad that my mum was in the room with us.'

The following day, the two brothers were brought to this boarding school. Their initial impressions of it was of a foreboding, scary place. It didn't help that they arrived in the evening, as it was getting dark. What sustained their sagging spirits a bit was the promise of seeing two older cousins, Paul and Niall, pupils at the school known to the two Fitzpatrick kids from holiday trips and visits for birthdays and other family occasions. As they approached Killashee's imposing, closed front door, Patrick and Francis began to think of Niall and Paul more as rescuers than as relatives.

Things got worse when the front door was opened by a nun in a dark habit. Francis had nothing against nuns. Neither did Patrick. They just didn't know what they were. In the mid-1960s, Hong Kong was a pretty colourful and exciting place, but nuns were thin on the ground. The particular nun who opened the door of the school to them was, as both remember it, very pleasant. Very, very pleasant. But that cut no ice with either of them. Just the thought of a nun scared them. A pleasant face at the top of all this full-length black robe wasn't enough to change the overall impression, which was terrifying.

Other nuns appeared, joining the one who had opened the door. Over the rustling of the habits and the noise of rosary beads hanging from the waist, the two little boys could hear the sisters saying 'Oh, your cousins are here'. Next thing, the cousins had arrived and the newcomers and the old hands were playing together. Threat beginning to recede, possibility of happiness returning.

Then the worst happened. It happened quickly and decisively.

'One of the nuns then grabbed me and showed me around,' Francis remembers. 'I burst into tears and I just wanted my mum and I went into a tantrum I think which was a horrible, horrible moment and then my mum was gone.'

He can't remember the details of his mother's departure. Only the distress of it and his own disbelief at finding himself in a cold, dark, monochrome place which smelled completely different to the way Hong Kong had smelled. In this new place, nuns in black with just a frill of white around the face surrounded him and told him he'd be grand and led him down endless corridors to strange rooms filled with more new faces and more black-garbed nuns.

'My mother was just gone,' Francis says bleakly about that day. 'I think the nun wouldn't let her say goodbye. You know the way they used to believe it would just make it worse for the child? Suddenly we were marched up to bed. I was just sobbing uncontrollably and did for the next week at least. It was a horrible, horrible experience. I have been lonely since but never to a crushing level of helplessness and isolation. My brother was there but he might as well have been on another planet. Everything I'd grown up with was stripped away from me and I was in this foreign country.'

Looking at my own five children, I shiver at the thought that any one of them would have such an experience. Yet, at that time, it was standard practice not just to send children to boarding school (and boarding schools were very different, back then) but for the parents to slip away without explanation. They did the best they knew how and, four decades later, Francis would chill you with his memories of how acutely, utterly and hopelessly lonely he was. Although, typical of Francis, he insists on interpreting it as a long-term positive factor. He feels he went through a crucible and came out stronger. I'm just glad that he didn't come out harder.

His mother visited the two boys as often as she could. Parting from her, at the end of her first visit, about three months after the two boys were enrolled in the school, he remembers as less excruciating.

'The worst of it was over then,' he says. 'Although it was very hard going back after Christmas, we were getting used to it.'

What he was getting used to was what he assumes prison is like: total regimentation. The pupils were subject to all sorts of rules and disciplines and wore a uniform. Inevitably, many of the children responded to the loneliness as if what they were experiencing was conscious child abuse. They became bed-wetters. Francis, who had just turned six in January and was put into the school in September, remembers the nuns trying to teach the boys to have control of their bladders and kidneys by not allowing them to go to the toilet on demand during lessons.

'They wouldn't let you go to the loo during class. They tried to train you so that you could go at breaks because otherwise you'd have, I suppose, all the kids going to the loo all the time. I just remember, I think we were saying the Angelus and I couldn't hold myself any longer and the teacher, she was very nice – Miss O'Shea, she was my first teacher – cleaned up for me …'

Francis is firmly convinced that no cruelty was intended by the nuns. The wisdom of the day dictated how they regulated the lives of the children in their care. Just as the wisdom of today dictates how we bring up the children in our care. You just have to hope that what we regard as perfectly acceptable doesn't look, in times to come, as bleak and harsh as the regimes of the past …

It wasn't all ghastly. Some of the rules and regulations suited Francis then – and suit him now. For example, the school gave its pupils no choice about religious services. You had to go to mass. You had to say the rosary. Francis sees both as good things which he has come back to very much in the last ten years. So, while the rest of us may shake our heads about his childhood, he maintains he has mostly happy memories of the time in school. It was, he says, good for him.

'It gave me an ability to get on with people,' he says. 'I got on well with the other kids – once I stopped sobbing! Once the emotional trauma subsided I made friends very quickly – some of those kids are still friendly with me. Plus, I learned my sports there. Sports were always, and still are, my favourite pastime.

It's perhaps just as well that Francis doesn't make a big deal of his early unhappiness, because there wasn't much evidence for it at the time. An aunt of his was the doctor for Killashee school. The fact that this aunt lived close to the school was a key reason the boys were sent there. Her name was Kitty Purcell. Dr Purcell reported to Francis' mother how the boys were doing. In recent days, when Francis tackled his mum on this issue – largely because he wants to send our own kids to Clongowes, another boarding school – his mother was startled by his reported misery. She said she never knew it had caused him so much distress because the word back from his aunt was that he was out playing football every day and enjoying himself. Certainly, sport and companionship turned the school experience positive fairly quickly, although neither could erase the memories of those first two years.

He also came around to the nuns of La Sainte Unione – a French order. Although the sisters are not in Killashee today, since it has been transformed into a luxury hotel, they are still in Ireland, based now in Athlone.

'They're wonderful,' Francis says. 'Their devotion to the kids, to us, was unbelievable. They took the vow of poverty seriously at all times, but they deprived themselves even further to build the sports hall for us – and that sports hall made such a difference to kids like me. They saved for years, having promised that they would build it, and it finally went up in my last year so I had a year of it. This wasn't achieved by sponsorship or fundraising like we're used to today. It was their own personal money that went into it. Apparently they saved all the money that they got as teachers to build the sports hall.'

Even though Francis is unguardedly honest about how destructive the early days of boarding school were for him, the overall experience was good, and he feels that if Daniel, George and Patrick (our own boys), go to Clongowes, the experience will be even better for them.

For starters, they'll only be twenty miles away from home and they'll be able to come home virtually every weekend if they wish. It's interesting, too, to listen to other kids who are from the area going to schools like Castleknock. You quickly learn that the kids actually want to stay in boarding school during the week. They quite like the regimentation. I suppose it's easier to be regimented by a large group of teachers, rather than your own parents, and to be regimented among friends, rather than coming home and believing all your friends have an easier time. Whatever the reason, it's a total reversal of the patterns of the past. A happy reversal.

By the time Francis was seven or eight, he had grown fond of Killashee. The place now felt enough like a home to him that he was actually quite upset leaving it when, at the age of twelve, in 1972, it was time to move on.

Not that there hadn't been movement in the six years he was there. He and his brother trundled back and forth to Hong Kong and Pakistan in the school holidays. His father had been posted to Karachi in Pakistan after Hong Kong, so Francis was a world traveller since birth. He loved every bit of it, which I find funny today, because he loathes travelling now. It's not just 'been there, done that', it's also because he truly hates being away from his children. And me. And his wider family. Of his eight siblings, apart from two who live in Florida, the other six, and his parents as well, live within a radius of perhaps twenty miles of our farm. Family members see each other more than they might have expected, back when the brothers were encountering the sisters only on school holidays.

When he was twelve, Francis did the entrance exam for Clongowes, the big Jesuit college in Kildare. Why Clongowes? Because his mother's family had gone there for generations. Plus, his mother's uncle, Fr Gerard O'Beirne, was a Jesuit in Clongowes. The Fitzpatricks may have been world travellers from birth, but when it came to secondary schooling, only one location would do: Clongowes. Unless, of course, any of them failed the entrance exam but thankfully, they all got it. I say 'thankfully' because if you push the button marked 'Clongowes', Francis makes like a human brochure for the place. He'd had a couple of peeks at it down through the years when he went to visit older cousins there, and his parents had done a pretty good job of persuading him that it was the best school in the world. When he went there, it lived up to the advance publicity.

'It had acres and acres of green fields for rugby, soccer, tennis, cricket,' he says, starting, as Francis always does, with sport. 'It had an indoor swimming pool. It had its own golf course. Food was exceptional.'

What startled him about Clongowes was the fact that, for the first couple of months there, all those kids that hadn't been to boarding school before, found it really hard, whereas for Francis, it was a breeze.

'I loved it. It was a holiday camp. It was just everything that Killashee wasn't. There was discipline but there was no uniform. Mass was optional, there was no rosary. Games were entirely at your own discretion. We were encouraged to participate, but you could choose what you wanted to play – soccer, rugby, swimming, you had your own time. It was great.'

Many people have a negative view of the Jesuit order, but Francis has nothing but good to say about them and the school where he encountered them.

'Clongowes was a place that committed you to be the very best you could be, but not at the expense of others. So there was a caring ethos there.'

It didn't help Francis' early street cred with the other students that he was chosen by the priests to be the sacristan. It was the last thing a guy who was into sports and socialising wanted to be because of the implication that the

71

sacristan – who helps the priest with mass, preparing his vestments, lighting the candles and carrying gifts up to the altar – has to be a Holy Joe.

'The rest of the kids gave me an awful slagging about it. It was the very last thing I needed but I just wasn't able to say no. Why did the priests pick me? I suppose they must have thought I was religious. The terrible thing was how eagerly I walked into it. What happened was that the priest who was our tennis coach came to me and said "There's a special job for you." I thought it was something to do with tennis and said "OK, do I get extra coaching or what?" He says "No, I want you, you're a very special boy, I want you to be the sacristan."'

The sacristan's role was not without its advantages. It was a job with perks. You were allowed extra time to play and you were treated as a prefect. Francis would have seen it as a complete win/win if it hadn't been for the way it established him in the minds of his peers as holier than them. This he would have found difficult to deal with if it hadn't been for his love of sports and skill on the playing field. In boys' schools, you get a free pass if you're good at sports, and Francis got a free pass on the piety perception.

Where he very decidedly did not get a free pass was when he broke ranks with his team and went on the mitch. To this day, he colours when this is mentioned. He sees it as a cross he has to live with and totally deserves.

Clongowes, at the time, was aiming to be the rugby school in Ireland. It wasn't quite making it. Not at rugby. In other sports, no problem. When it came to tennis, Clongowes would win all the Leinster championships. Swimming, the school was good at. Cricket, they were quite good at.

But as Francis went through the years from 1972 to 1978 everything was focused in on rugby and that was the period that laid the foundations for the great rugby school Clongowes is, right now. A new coach came in – Fr Michael Shiels from Belvedere. He did the impossible. After fifty-two years Clongowes won the final of the Leinster Senior Schools Championship, beating Terenure, the hot favourites in the final.

'No, I wasn't actually on the team. I played in the backs, which was quite unusual because I was a tall guy and big so I should really have been a forward but because I was very skilful at soccer you develop skills in rugby that are quite unusual for a big guy. Big guys play the forwards and then smaller guys play the backs but I was kind of unusual. I wasn't on the team and they won without me so I can have no qualms on that – I didn't deserve to be on it. What happened was I was on the thirds team the year before, in 1977, and I made one of the worst decisions ever. There was horse racing at Punchestown and I decided to let my team down and go off because a friend of mine had been offered a lift to the races and horse racing is my passion. So I asked another friend to cover for me because if he'd covered they'd hardly have known I was missing: I was playing second centre that day and you don't get much ball in that position anyway. Unfortunately, something happened – he couldn't make it, so it was fourteen players against fifteen.'

Francis was in serious trouble. He was thrown off the rugby squad which meant that he couldn't try out for a place on the team going forward. He was totally excluded, felt grievously ashamed and to this day is mortified because he believes that he handled the whole episode abominably. He wishes he'd gone in immediately with his hands up, asking for forgiveness and apologising.

'I did apologise in due course, but they still felt that I was in severe breach of discipline. So I spent sixth year in Clongowes watching the other guys train.'

Francis had experienced isolation and loneliness before,

but what made this worse was that he had brought it on himself. He didn't like the enforced loner status. But he didn't pretend to be cool about it. Nor does he shrug it off today.

'I can't blame the guy who promised to cover for me because something happened that was completely outside of his control. No. It was my fault. The isolation, though. It was so painful. All my friends were on this team. Dozens of girls from all the girls schools were at all the matches because these were heroes. The Leinster Cup. It was superstardom, it was the limelight, it was everything a hormone-filled young boy could ever have dreamed of and I was there and I was part of it but isolated. I was just totally isolated and it's something I haven't come to terms with yet. It still causes me grief. Still. In one sense I'm well over it but we all have our childhood dreams and mine was to be on that team.'

Like a man touching a sore tooth with his tongue, Francis, even now, makes the experience – in my view – more painful than he needs to, by reminding himself that he could have been on that team. He proved it to himself – heaven alone knows why – the following year, when a lot of the boys who were on the Clongowes team went to Belvedere for the under 19s. Of course the former outcast was allowed to play then. Belvedere welcomed him with open arms. He went out and proved to himself: 'not to anyone else but just to myself that I should have been on that team.'

I'm always struck by how like *Aesop's Fables* Francis' stories of his childhood are. They all have a lesson that he was supposed to learn. A lesson that in most cases he has learned and learned the hard way. But sometimes, they have an odd postscript to them, too. This one, for example, has more than one moral. There's 'don't let down your team-mates'. There's 'When you do wrong, 'fess up quickly and apologise, big-time.' There's 'Take your punishment like a man and don't pretend you're not suffering or that you didn't deserve it.' But at the end of all of the morals, there's the postscript.

'Of course, if I had been on that team,' goes Francis' postscript, 'it would have used up a lot of the energy and drive that I have now. Because if I look at the heroes of that team, they've done well in life but I've also done OK. That, in a sense, is one of the driving forces in my life. I hope to make up to myself for that pain of being left out.'

Francis brought three key traits with him from Killashee: a passion for sport, neatness in handwriting and in organising homework, and diligence. Not brilliance. He never claims that. He is, he says, an average student. In fact, he's very good at languages and got a good leaving certificate – not quite good enough to get him into law, which is where he decided he wanted to go, but he did the matric and that launched him into law.

Getting into law was a generational dream for the Fitzpatricks. Francis' father had always wanted to be a lawyer, but his parents hadn't been able to afford to send him to university when he was growing up. Still, he never pushed the idea on his sons, always being the kind of man to encourage each of his children to do the best they could at whatever they chose for themselves.

And so, Francis began his law degree in UCD in Belfield. The context was markedly in contrast with what he had been used to in Clongowes. It was the first time he'd ever sat beside a girl in class. Now, Francis has four sisters, so the girl thing wasn't completely new to him. What *was* completely new to him was dealing with girls other than his sisters. No one had ever told him how you deal with a girl, how you talk to them.

'We had been to what we called "social events" but I had no girlfriends,' he confesses. 'I was very naïve. I had no idea how to deal with the female lawyers. The only thing I remember is that I made this decision: You don't ever want to marry a lawyer. It sounds like some mad prejudice, particularly because, sitting to the right and left of me down through the following years were some very nice girls. I just always felt I wouldn't like to have to discuss work at home or something.'

You especially wouldn't want to be discussing work at home if you hated it, and Francis quickly found he loathed law. He found it terribly boring. Also at that time, he was doing very well at sports. Remember the short-lived battle at Killashee between sport and music? Think re-play. With sport winning again. Except this time the consequences were serious. Francis failed first year law.

Oddly, it didn't help that he was – for virtually the first time since his toddler years – living at home, and loving it. He cherished every moment with his family, who were delighted to have him around. The hidden disadvantage, of course, was that this was a family which had never had to enforce homework times. They had no concept of how a student should actually study. Consequently, they were both amazed and disappointed when Francis came a cropper at his first academic fence.

'They couldn't believe it. Here was their Clongowes-educated boy and he failed. I was always a good enough student and never caused any trouble. I felt I let them down. I felt gutted for myself, but much more for them. I was very embarrassed. To repeat in those days! I think nothing of it now but that's because I know that some of the best lawyers including the best senior and junior counsel were the guys who failed law with me, that first year. The guys who fail are the practical guys because they're doing other things and having girlfriends as well.'

Francis maintains, at least to me, that girlfriends were

not a major contributory factor in his first year failure. He portrays himself as a bit of a slow starter in that department. It didn't add to his confidence that, in addition to failing law, he was dropped from the soccer team as well. It just wasn't a good year.

In his repeat year, he joined Fine Gael 'because friends were in it' but went to only one or two meetings and then dropped out. Later that year, he want to the beer festival in Munich, thanks to a man named Bobby Howick who was quite famous at the time as the face of Guinness. Howick's son, Peter, and Francis were pals, and Mr Howick got them a job in Munich that summer. Francis had learned German during his repeat year, and so arrived in Munich with fair fluency. He enjoyed every minute of it. He was living away from home but living on his own terms, with his pals, earning his own money, in a big city.

'We had no restrictions and no mothers,' is the way he sums it up. 'We could do what we wanted.'

That's precisely what they did, and had a great time doing it. It helped that they were suddenly rich. Perhaps not rich by the standards of fulltime workers, but they were paid £150 a week, could live on £20 a week and so could buy whatever they wanted and do whatever they wanted. It was a happy time.

Afterwards, Francis returned to college and concentrated on studying. The exams were tough, particularly when he had progressed to Blackhall Place, where a fifty per cent failure rate for top law students was the average. The prospect of failing at that point changed everything. Just as Dr Johnson said that the prospect of being hanged in the morning will concentrate a man's mind wonderfully, the possibility of failing after so much time and money had been invested in a law career concentrated Francis' mind wonderfully.

Not until he was doing his postgraduate diploma in UCD, at the age of twenty-five, did he have a girlfriend. At that point, he got seriously involved for the first time in what turned out to be a three-year relationship.

'She broke up with me,' he confesses. 'I was quite hurt by that because I always, in my own mind, felt that she was more dispensable than I was. Hell of a shock and did me good. But it was a terrible time. It taught me humility. It taught me to respect other people. I hadn't respected her as much as I should have.'

Geographical distance had contributed to his lack of respect. The girl was in Dublin. Francis, for much of their relationship, was in Brussels as a stagiere (trainee); this is a prestigious appointment reserved for European and international graduates allowing them six months paid work experience with the European Commission in Brussels.

'I was in Brussels having the time of my life,' he remembers. 'To have my girlfriend in Dublin was brilliant. I wasn't married. I was messing around in Brussels. There were lovely European girls and I really hadn't much thought for her other than it was nice to have her at home. When I went home it was great, which was very unfair to her. She didn't know how I felt ... but anyway I was quite shocked when she gave me the bullet.'

He probably would have coped with the unexpected but instructive humiliation, except that, about a month later, a close friend of his, John Fay, was killed in a car crash. The combination of shocks happened at a time when Francis wasn't ready for them. Physically or emotionally. The life of a stagiere, as he had been living it, was six months of free booze and food laced with cream. He had gone from thirteen to nineteen stone in three months.

'That September, 1987, my mother didn't recognise me at the airport. My hair was grey, not totally grey, but certainly grey around the temples. I had gone out to Brussels as a supremely fit young man because I was boxing in college when I was doing my postgraduate work.'

Ironically, Francis had taken up boxing in the first place at John's urging. John had not only been a keen boxer, but a fine one: British and Irish middle-weight champion. John convinced Francis that the cure for the boredom Francis experienced doing a too-easy apprenticeship was boxing. Although Francis is non-violent by natural instinct, he nonetheless loved boxing and was supremely fit when heading out to Brussels.

But he hooked up with the wrong crowd in Brussels, becoming pals with guys who were there to doss at the expense of the taxpayer.

On his arrival home, his mother was so shocked at his appearance that she immediately brought him to the doctor, who took one look at him and announced that he had never seen such a transformation. Nor was the problem simply one of appearance. The doctor's records showed that when Francis had been examined in his office just before he left for Brussels, he had one of the lowest heartbeats ever and was in fantastic shape.

'You are going to kill yourself inside of six months if you don't change your lifestyle,' said the GP.

Francis moved back to Brussels, dealt with the death of his friend and changed his lifestyle. He was still depressed.

'That twin experience with the loss of a relationship and the death of a friend was quite a pincer movement on the emotions,' is how he sums it up today.

It took him time to recover. Another lawyer friend of his advised him that if he wanted to get fit quickly, karate was the way to go. He took up karate and in three months had lost all the excess weight. Today, he talks with pleasure about being 'back in supreme fighting condition'. That capacity to fiercely, almost combatively, embrace a punishing regime is typical of Francis. It's not that he finds any fun in being disciplined, but he's convinced that discipline creates fun, creates a good lifestyle and gives you satisfaction.

'When you've nothing to get up for except another party, there's no incentive. Looking back, I know the unhappiest time of my life was in Brussels and I have never gone back since.'

Even though he was now taking charge of his life again, the trailing malaise of the six months of disorganisation affected his performance at job interviews set up for him in London. At the first couple of interviews he was very good, but at the final interviews in each firm, it just wasn't in him to push for the appointment or present himself in any driving way. He knew himself that Brussels had nearly killed him and he feared that if, at that point, he got a well-paid job too easily, he simply would not have the discipline to look after himself away from home. His instinct, at twenty-seven, was to get back to Dublin, even if it meant accepting a salary which was a third of what was on offer in London. So back he came to a job in commercial law and a modest salary cheque.

It was a better decision than he could have known at the time. London was then coming to the end of the Thatcher boom. The British economy was about to turn very sour indeed, with the result that those guys and girls who, fresh out of Brussels, snapped up high-paying jobs in London, were all fired after three to four months.

Dublin, for the next two years, represented a hard but productive re-entry for a man in his twenties who had been cock-of-the-walk in Brussels. Soon, having used karate to return to the fitness he always craves, he was playing soccer again, and his law firm quickly realised that not only could he do the work but he was also very good at being with clients and was bringing in decent money for the firm. In no time at all, he was being head-hunted. The firm he was with increased his pay packet and told him the company would pay for whatever new car he would like for himself. He went out and bought a jet black Alpha Romeo 33 TI, a car being marketed at the time as 'passion on wheels'.

The company was a highly professional niche law firm. He liked the people and stayed there for five years before leaving to set up on his own. That was a major watershed for him. Once you start your own practice, you sink or swim. He swam. Plus, his social life was the best it had been for a long time, not least because his sister, Patricia, was in Ryanair, a new kind of airline, which allowed him to meet a lot of air hostesses.

He also fell in love with a girl from Canada. She was based in Montreal. Francis was based in Dublin. A little like the situation when he'd been in Brussels and his then girlfriend was back in Ireland, he was able to use what he still cherishes as the greatest chat-up line: 'My girlfriend's in Montreal.' It meant that you weren't available. But you might be. There was no pressure on the girl you were chatting up, because you were already spoken for. Francis claims that, as a marketing approach, it was phenomenal, delivering nearly one hundred per cent of the time, to the astonishment of his friends.

'I was in great shape, I was fit and at this stage of my life I'd stopped drinking completely. I had decided to give drink a miss. It wasn't St Paul on the road to Damascus situation – I can't even tell you why I did it – maybe it was for fitness. But it worked. I was never tired because I wasn't drinking. My friends loved me because I would collect them all and chauffeur them around and the enjoyment I got out of it was way in excess of what they thought they were getting.'

He was living with a cousin, Tony O'Beirne, who was also

a good friend of his. They shared a house in Terenure. Francis would see his girlfriend perhaps twice a year. His new firm – the one he had set up himself – was located in Dublin, in Mount Street, opposite the Fine Gael office and just down the street from the Fianna Fáil office.

On the face of it, things could hardly have been better for Francis Fitzpatrick, owner of a little black book filled with girlfriends' names. Beneath all the socialising, however, he was beginning to develop a niggling sense that something was missing. Or, to put it simply: how long could he party?

It was around that time that he met me. Six months later, everything had changed and the two of us were talking to a priest about the wedding. Or, rather, about what the priest insisted we go through *before* the wedding.

Chapter Six

STARVATION AND SLEEP DEPRIVATION

A few years ago, the Catholic Church in Ireland – and for all I know, in other countries, too – decided that young couples needed to more fully understand the depth of the commitment they were undertaking in marriage. Pre-marriage courses had always existed, but participation, for the most part, was a matter of personal choice. If the two of you wanted to attend such a course, you did. If you found the prospect off-putting, you didn't.

Then the Church got tough, letting engaged couples know that the Church's involvement in the ceremony was more than the 'rent of the hall' for the day. Having your wedding in a Catholic church became contingent on attending a pre-marriage course.

This was explained to Francis and me by Fr Gleason, my local parish priest from Skryne. We indicated that, because of my job in England, there was simply no way I could join Francis in Dublin on the days necessary to fulfil the requirement. Fr Gleason thought about this for a while: 'Could ye do a weekend?' he asked.

We nodded.

'Good,' he said. 'If ye can do a weekend, ye can do Lough Derg.'

Francis got all enthusiastic, thinking this was a real let-off from the pre-marriage course. I was a bit less enthusiastic, not knowing much about it.

St Patrick's Purgatory, Lough Derg, about forty miles north of Pettigo in County Donegal, has been a place of pilgrimage for more than a thousand years. It's a place of voluntary suffering and personal re-discovery through fasting and sleep deprivation. During the thirteenth and fourteenth centuries, it was known throughout Europe and pilgrims would come from afar to visit the island in the lake. Legend has it that the 'Derg' in the placename derives from the Irish word 'red' and refers to the blood of the last great serpent, killed by St Patrick, who banished all snakes from Ireland.

People of all religions and of none are welcomed on the island, where they go barefoot for two nights of prayer and penance. The prayer takes pilgrims around the island to what are called penitential beds: circles of rough stones or boulders with a crucifix in the centre where you kneel. Each is dedicated to a particular saint.

Pilgrims arrive on the island between 11 a.m. and 3 p.m. on the first day of their pilgrimage, having fasted from midnight. They must stay awake, doing spiritual exercises for that twenty-four hours as part of the three-day pilgrimage, eating only one meal per day, that meal consisting of dry toast or oatcake with black tea or coffee.

This is what Fr Gleason decided would be the moral equivalent of a pre-marriage course for Francis and me. He was right, at least in the sense that if Francis and I could survive three starving days on a penitential island together without me braining him, we had a good chance of withstanding whatever trials life had to throw at us.

I'll never forget it. Never forget the cold, the hunger, the yearning for sleep. But, coming through all three was a growing certainty: this is the right man for me. Francis minded me and tried to keep me awake during those periods when the need to sleep became an agony. Fr Gleason, in his wisdom, picked a pre-marriage course that was slightly outside the norm, but was truly effective. When we were leaving the island, both of us had a sense of learned strength that would stand to us in the tough times ahead. Francis was so enthusiastic about the experience that he's done the pilgrimage since with friends and now brings a group every year. Once was enough for me. I believe that my pilgrimage is childbirth which I have been blessed to accomplish five times.

The other big pre-marriage test was telling my bosses in Smurfits what I was going to do, knowing that they would have a negative reaction. Not just negative, but astonished, because they had never had a warning that I might up and leave for marriage. If they looked at my past, I was always very committed to business and career: I was looked on as a career girl.

I remember walking into that office with fear and dread having to tell the news to Ray Newell, the man who had put his confidence in me and had said to me: 'don't let me down.' Here I was, coming to let him down. That was a tough meeting because he was mad.

'What are you going to do when you go back to Ireland?' he asked me. 'Have you really thought about it?'

'Maybe I could work for Smurfits again in Ireland?' I suggested.

'The only way you'd possibly do that is if you'd give us more time over here,' was his response.

'How about April,' I suggested and the suggestion lay there for a while. When April came, it was like starting the torturous procedure all over again.

'Will you give us a few more months?' he asked.

Again, I hung on for a little more, hoping that giving them the extra months would help me get a job at home with Smurfits. It was July before they released me. I went home to get ready for my wedding and to discuss career prospects in Ireland with Smurfits. But Smurfits closed the door on me. I was out of a job.

But I didn't panic. I didn't worry. I had to get ready for

my wedding. In addition, I had the support of Francis. I felt sad at the prospect of not continuing to work for the company, because I had done bloody well in Smurfits. I loved that company. I really did. I admired Michael Smurfit. I even had pictures up on the wall of the man. I idolised him. I thought he was brilliant. So even though I was out of the company, I wasn't bitter because they had given me a good grounding and I was confident that when the time was right, I could do quality control consultancy.

But planning for a business future was put on hold as we launched on the beginning of a whole new chapter in our lives. We got married on 6 October 1994. It was a fabulous day in my local church in Skryne for the marriage ceremony and then the Shelbourne Hotel for the reception afterwards. I never expect a man to describe a wedding as 'fairytale' or even think of it that way, but that's how Francis remembers it.

'Her sisters are all beautiful girls,' he tells people. 'My friends all thought they were very attractive. It was a fairytale wedding – I would say that of course …!'

The fairytale ground to a sudden halt when we arrived at the airport to fly out for our honeymoon in Playa del Carmen about sixty miles south of Cancun in Mexico. Up we went to the check-in desk.

'You've missed your flight,' the guy on the desk said.

We looked at him stupidly.

'You've missed your flight to London,' he said.

That didn't sound too bad.

'Missing your flight to London means you have also missed all of your connecting flights to Mexico,' he clarified.

It turned out that we had missed that first crucial outward flight because Francis misread our tickets. For a man who is so organised, it was an amazing and untypical mistake to make. He didn't read the first page which dealt with the flight from Ireland to England. Instead, he read the details of the flight from England to Texas, but he was reading it as the flight from Dublin.

'We're on our honeymoon,' Francis said.

The guy shrugged. Our being on honeymoon wasn't going to bring the planes back.

'We'll have to go home,' Francis said to me.

'We're going to London,' I told him. 'We'll think about it over there. I am not going home to say I didn't go on a honeymoon.'

By this point, half the airport had become aware of the honeymoon couple who'd missed their honeymoon flight. Suddenly, everybody became invested in solving our problem. The airlines in Dublin were unbelievably kind and accommodating to us as honeymooners. Ryanair, Aer Lingus and BA all offered to put us on their next flights at no charge to get us to London. After that, it was up to us.

We flew to London. There, we decided that we'd take the next day's flight over to Texas with a short hop down to Mexico. However, when we tried to get tickets, they wanted us to pay an additional £200 per person for missing the previous day's flight. We didn't have that much money to spare. So Francis turned to me: 'If you want the tickets,' he said severely, for the benefit of the booking agents, 'we'll have no spending money on our honeymoon.'

My eyes filled up with tears. Not because I was pretending, but because I was genuinely stricken at the thought of a honeymoon without the capacity to do even modest spending. The people at check-in softened.

'It's OK,' the girl behind the desk said, 'we'll do this as a gesture on the part of the company.'

We got on the flight with our cash still in our back pockets. I was in a confused state of relief. Francis was on a high. He says he knew from that moment on we were going to be a great team.

Our honeymoon was spent in one of those all-inclusive sun resorts. It was quite an experience. Francis' skin is super-sensitive to the sun whereas mine is not; I have good skin for a tan. The first day on honeymoon, I went rushing out into the sunshine as soon as possible with as little as possible on me, and promised to wait for Francis out of doors. Dumb-struck wasn't the word when he came down towards me on the beach and went in for a swim wearing long trousers, a white shirt and a white hat. He came out of the sea like a drowned rat in a theatrical costume. I was so ashamed. I couldn't believe he had planned to honeymoon in the scorching sun covered from head to toe in this white sea-going outfit.

'I have to stay out of the sun,' he said, as if swimming fully dressed was a minor variation on resort behaviour.

Here was me in my semi-naked best. Here was me with an assortment of beautiful bikinis. Here was me ready to be half a beautiful honeymoon couple. And here was Francis looking like a refugee thrown up by a tidal wave.

Now, of course, you will say that what Francis wore was his business, and I would have to agree with that. You might also say that he was perfectly entitled to preserve his health, and I wouldn't disagree on that, either. But at that age, I was very much into what would people think, so I was mortified by the expectation that they would all be looking at him and sniggering over his clothing.

In fact, his weird wardrobe taught me a lesson, which is that people don't care that much about you. People have their own lives and vanities and preoccupations which are much more important to them than you are. If you are worried at what people think about you or their perception of you, then you're wasting your time. After a couple of days with Francis in his unique beach-gear, I got used to it and had copped on to the self-absorption of the human species.

Francis might be afraid of the sun, with some justification, but he's not afraid of much else. Once we had settled into the resort, he decided he would like to take me out on the ocean in one of these abseiling laser boats. Because he didn't really know how to sail one, he decided to employ one of the locals. His chosen helper was a small, portly man, little enough to come up as far as Francis' waist, and who normally hired out the sail boats to experienced abseilers. Which we were not.

'If you give me a few lessons,' Francis told him, always ready to do a deal, 'I'll bring you down some food.'

This was a great offer, because the locals were very poor and the food within this all-in resort was flown in from America and it was lovely. The boatman indicated he would regard this as a good deal. However, we then discovered that it was part of the policy of the people in the resort not to give food away to people working on the beaches who, even if employed indirectly by the resort, had their own quarters. Francis now had an enthusiastic customer for food it was forbidden to provide him with. Not only that, but he couldn't re-negotiate the deal. The guy had made up his mind that he would do the job only if food was forthcoming.

Francis decided he would have to embark, if not on a life of crime, at least on a holiday of crime. Except the only way he could commit his crime was to get me involved. He also decided I would be a better collaborator if I was spared the details of the plot, and therefore didn't tell me anything about the resort policy against food-smuggling. I brought trailer-loads of beautiful food down to the beach in happy ignorance of the rules I was breaking. Nobody ever asked me what on earth I was carrying in my oversized beach bags, and my new husband behaved as casually as if he'd asked me to bring him a tube of fruit gums.

That was how Francis learned to abseil. Although I'm

not sure he'd have passed an abseiling exam. The first and only time he brought me out on the ocean, I actually thought I was going to die, right there, on my honeymoon, when it emerged that his lessons hadn't included giving him an understanding of how to turn the boat. This emerged just as the weather turned threatening.

First of all, the wind changed suddenly. Clouds gathered overhead. The water got blacker. Land looked further away, the figures on the beach no bigger than ants. I was panicking because I knew he didn't know how poor a swimmer I was. Francis was panicking because he knew if I knew how bad things were I'd die of fright.

Neither of us let on how scared we were until, however we managed it, we were back on land. At that point, it was easier to laugh than fight about it.

Chapter Seven

HERE'S A BOOK THAT'S ALL ABOUT YOU

After our honeymoon, we went to live in Skryne in County Meath, in an unoccupied house belonging to my parents. They wouldn't accept any rent from us. All we had to do was pay our own bills. I wasn't earning anything and Francis wasn't earning a lot but we weren't spending that much and were able to cope reasonably within our means. That was probably the only time we've ever managed to live within our means. Since then we've gone against the economics theory that Dickens espouses in (I think) *The Old Curiosity Shop*. Mr Gradgrind says that all economics is the following: income 19s 6d – expenditure 20s – disaster. Income 20s – expenditure 19s – 6d happiness. We've managed to outspend our earnings most of the time and still end up in profit on the bottom line of happiness.

I went through the logistics of setting up my own consultancy but I was in no rush to go out and push for business, having learned of the 'lead time' between doing a consultancy job and getting paid for it. In addition, I had other priorities. My parents had given me a site as a wedding present so I could build a house. That incorporated two acres and we decided to buy the five acres beside it from my dad just to have a little bit extra. We were planning, if we got lucky, to have children straight away. I'm from a family of nine, Francis is from a family of eight, so we were both attuned to the idea of having several children.

I was full of drive and energy and the fact that my career was on hold didn't bother me much. Francis was more conflicted about it. He felt that in selling himself to me as my husband, he had made me compromise my career because Smurfits wouldn't let me back to Dublin. He was big on the bible story which was 'give up everything, come follow me and you shall inherit the earth'. I didn't take that literally, but he still felt that if he could get me something that would make as much money and give as much prestige as my Smurfit job had given, that it would be a nice payback. So he was constantly on the lookout for the perfect opportunity to get my career moving again.

He himself was specialising in one aspect of the law, believing that niche expertise is always better than general competence. The area he chose, and became expert in, was franchise law. This was why, in January or February of the year after we got married, he went to a franchise exhibition.

At the exhibition, he encountered a Londoner named Mike Parsons, a fast-talking classic salesman. Francis thought he was great fun. But Mike is also an Eastender and, therefore, focused on the sale. So when the two of them had enjoyed a few jokes, Mike cut to the chase: 'This is a great business,' he said, gesturing at the display behind him. 'Francis, you should buy it.'

'Hold on a second,' Francis said. 'I'm a lawyer. I don't need to buy a franchise.'

'You're gonna lose money if you don't,' Mike retorted.

He didn't have to prove his point. It was perfectly obvious to Francis that this display was getting more interest from the people attending the exhibition than any other stand. The product Mike was offering, called Personalised Books, didn't sound terribly attractive, but the attention it was getting persuaded Francis to ask a lot of questions and to seek a sample from Mike to take away with him.

When Francis arrived home that evening, he made no mention of the exhibition, just casually dropped a hardback book on the mantelpiece where I came upon it a little later. It was a children's book about a character named Freya. Since Francis has a niece he adores named Freya, I thought: 'What an interesting coincidence.' As I began to read the text, I found out that it wasn't just the character's first name that matched Francis' niece. The surname matched, too. The character was named Freya Hickey.

'Hey, Francis,' I said. 'Where did you get this book?'

'Oh,' he said, ultra-casual, 'It's just something I picked up somewhere.'

He didn't even look up from the papers he was working on.

'How is it all about Freya Hickey, your niece?' I demanded.

He shrugged, still preoccupied – ostensibly – with the paperwork.

'I don't know. Must happen now and again that there's a book out there about you, using your name.'

I digested this and then rejected it. Whatever about a book based around a name like John Smith, It was a chance in a billion that by pure coincidence a book would centre on such an unusual name as Freya Hickey. I was intrigued. Francis, meanwhile, betrayed no interest in the book at all. It was just something he had spotted and brought home. Now, he had more important things to do. He said nothing about it for the whole evening. The first time he made an oblique reference to it was the following morning.

'By the way,' he asked, all casual and routine. 'D'you want that business?'

'What business?' I responded, mystified. 'What are you talking about?'

'That business where you could make books for people using the names of their children,' he said, as if it was obvious.

I went back to where I had put down the book about

Freya. It was incredibly impressive, because it was so professionally done. It was a hardback book printed in full colour throughout, with an interesting story to it. But I still couldn't get my head around the concept of 'personalised publishing'.

'Look, the books come in packages,' Francis explained. 'So let's say you have a book already written about, say, the teddy bears' picnic. Right?'

I nodded. That far, I was with him.

'What you do is this. You insert the name of the child in that title, in the software that makes up that title. It fills that name into the plot wherever it should, you simply print out and bind the book, and that's it – a fairytale completely written about your daughter or your son or your niece or your nephew. They're at the teddy bears' picnic. You can truthfully say to them, "Here's a book that's all about you"!'

'What child could resist that?' I wondered aloud.

There were, he added, some twenty different titles in the range and whichever title you chose, the book could be altered so that it would be all about yourself on that day. There was even a book for little sports fans, which allowed the young reader to play with their favourite team.

'This is a business I spotted at the franchise exhibition,' Francis said.

'What do you mean, a business?' I asked.

'Making personalised books,' he said. 'You have a computer with the story in it. Then a customer comes along and you insert their name and their child's name and the story wraps around those names so they become the characters. The software prints the whole thing out, you bind it, and what you have is a completely personalised book you can charge for. I thought you might find it interesting to buy the master franchise for Ireland and run it as a business.'

'Where?' I asked.

'Where what?'

'Where can I buy this?' I asked.

'You want to?'

'Of course I want to.'

'Right now?'

'Of course!'

'Let's go, then.'

We hopped into the car and Francis drove straight back to the O'Reilly Hall in UCD where he had originally spotted the books. The price for the franchise was £10,000 sterling, which of course we didn't have. But was that going to stop us? Not a chance. As far as I was concerned, it was another slice of destiny. I could enjoy doing this and make money at it. Therefore, Francis' job was just to buy that business for me.

He, of course, was chuffed that the idea he had spotted had clicked so comprehensively with me. Off he went to the Ulster Bank: 'I've just bought a business,' he told them. 'I need £10k sterling.'

They looked at him as if he had two heads.

'Francis, you're a lawyer,' they said. 'You just can't go out and buy a business.'

'But I have bought it for my wife, she's a senior executive, can you guys give us the cash?'

'How much cash?'

'£12,000 punts.'

'Oh God no, we can't give you that amount of money.'

'Well that's fine,' Francis said, furious with them. 'I'll get it from Bank of Ireland.'

When he went to Bank of Ireland it was the same story – 'you're a lawyer, what are you doing buying a business? Your wife is a senior executive, she knows nothing about this new business.'

In order not to let the franchise slip out of our hands, Francis had to – for the first time – do something he got into the habit of doing later: ringing a friend and asking for money. He telephoned his brother-in-law, Ciaran Hickey, described the business and explained it was me who would be operating it. Ciaran, who had sold his business around that time and had some spare cash, gave Francis the loan we needed to get the venture started.

Within two days of Francis spotting the books at that exhibition, we had bought the franchise for Ireland. We had no background in publishing, but we had complete confidence that this was going to take off, that this was an idea whose time had come, that this was a product that was really going to work. Of course, just as we hadn't the money when we decided to take a chance on personalised publishing, we didn't have a venue, either. But we floated along in the belief that this thing was a sure-fire winner.

My task, as soon as we had signed the contract and paid upfront for the equipment, was to get a location. The obvious choice was Dublin, where we figured that any of the shopping malls would be perfect. We had, of course, no inkling as to the cost of space in a popular shopping mall.

We first went to the Ilac Centre, but the rents were too colossal to justify the expenditure. I went into a few of the shopping centres around the outskirts and then decided to go into Stephen's Green. There, I met a man named Michael Stokes, the manager of the complex. I went into his office and sold him on the concept, which he thought was brilliant. He showed me around all the rental shops, telling me the rents as we walked. You were talking about £20,000 for rent on the bottom floor. It's a lot more now but even at that time I couldn't justify it at all. By the time we got to the third floor, I was walking very slowly, squashed by the prices.

'I'm really sorry, Denise,' he said. 'I can't really help you, we don't have anything free at the kind of price you can pay.'

'I wouldn't need much space,' I said aloud. 'It's only a

computer and I'd ...' I faltered, because I couldn't really work out how I could do what I wanted to do.

'Well, I'll tell you what,' Michael said. 'You walk around yourself and if you find an area that you think will work, I'll have a look.'

With that, he left me and headed back to his own suite. I went around that shopping centre again and again and again. I looked everywhere.

Eventually, up on the third floor, beside the car park entrance into the management suite, I found a ten-foot corner. I went back into Michael's office.

'You found something?'

He looked surprised.

'I found the perfect spot,' I told him and gestured him to follow me to the little corner I had located.

'What I could do is this,' I said. 'I'll close it off and I'll have a place that I could put my computer and till.'

I couldn't believe it when he said yes. Then it came to rent and the best word to describe what he proposed was minuscule. We shook hands on it before he could have second thoughts. It was March around Paddy's Day and I had a location. In no time at all I had my whole set-up installed: a little press, a fold-up table, a till and an ordinary computer-cum-printer.

This is how it worked. You'd give me your child's name and address, together with the names of two of the child's friends and I would incorporate the information in a book which becomes a gift from mammy and daddy and is a keepsake. There was no selling on it. Once the people came over, they were sold immediately. They could see it was brilliant and great for presents. It quickly confirmed our judgement that it was a good franchise to go for, and it turned into a solid business.

Nonetheless, that first year was very hard because I became pregnant as well. I had to get there early in the morning, fighting my way through clouds of morning sickness and stay there all day in constant contact with customers and with the computer. It wasn't impossible, but it required attention and energy, so it was tough. The fact that it was tough did not detract from the modest profits we were already making and from the realisation that this was a fran-chise with enormous potential. It helped, too, that I was getting what could be called 'instant money', compared with working as a consultant, where you might not get the fee for the job you did for ninety days or even longer.

The big breakthrough for us was the *Live at Three* afternoon television programme presented by Thelma Mansfield and Derek Davis. They were out and about looking for women in business and they did a five-minute slot with me. The item went out, if I remember rightly, in April 1996. Literally the minute it aired, the Stephen's Green Shopping Centre phonelines went down under the pressure of calls. Talk about the power of (free) advertising. Suddenly, we weren't just doing good business, we were doing *phenomenal* business. The Stephen's Green Centre management insisted that we got our own phone because they were inundated with people looking for us. They weren't looking for us by our name though, they were looking for a character named Piggley Pooh, whose picture they had seen in the footage during *Live at Three*.

Piggley Pooh got his first break on television through a series of accidents. Before the television programme came along, sales had been walking into our tiny corner of the shopping centre in sufficient numbers to justify setting up a limited company. The two of us kicked around a lot of possibilities before a character from my childhood surfaced, unexpectedly, outside Leinster House. The two of us were in Francis' car, stuck in traffic, outside the dáil (Irish house of parliament) one day, when I noticed a fat baldy guy driving a convertible with the roof down a few cars ahead of us.

'Isn't he a real Piggley Pooh?' I giggled.

Francis looked all around him, mystified.

'Your man in the convertible,' I said, nodding towards it.

Francis looked at the guy.

'Well, OK,' he said equably. 'But who's Piggley Pooh?'

'Oh, you *know* Piggley Pooh,' I started to say, and then realised he couldn't know Piggley Pooh. To Francis, this character from my childhood, a character enmeshed with every braincell I own, was just a funny conglomeration of syllables.

As the traffic started to move, and the human Piggley Pooh began to pull away from us, I explained to Francis that Piggley Pooh was a pig I saw in my grandmother's every time I went down to visit her. By the time we were out of Hume Street, I was telling him about me playing out in the hay on my own and actually imagining Piggley Pooh scuttling in and out. It was the first time Francis had heard my Piggley Pooh stories.

At that stage, I had never written any of my stories down. Never put any of them on paper. I'd never had an urge to type them out or show them to anyone else. They were all in my head and all intertwined with my life experiences. I started to explain this to Francis, but he was somewhat distracted by the name of my main character.

'Piggley Pooh,' he murmured, giving it an extra syllable.

'No,' I said. 'Not Piggilly, just Piglee.'

'It's a great name,' he said.

'Isn't it?'

'Be a great name for the book company.'

In the beginning, we had first called our company Rainbow Books. Neither of us had been satisfied with it, it was too vague, too happy-slappy. It never really conjured up what we were trying to do.

'That's what we'll do,' I now said, 'We'll call ourselves the Piggley Pooh company.'

The name sounded pleasing, was easy to remember, and sounded as if it linked with a children's product. It didn't matter to the purchasers of our personalised books what the company name was but I was delighted with the idea. While I'd never turned the original Piggley into a pet – the George Clooney fashion for pet pigs came too late for me – that piglet was like a childhood little friend I'd grown up with. Hence the great pull the name had for me.

Once we had decided that Piggley Pooh was going to come out of anonymity in Skryne and get his chance at stardom in the Stephen's Green Centre, I had to go and get him immortalised visually. Since we were setting up a company in his name and would require a logo, the best option would be to base the logo on the character. I had to describe what Piggley Pooh looked like to an artist so he could make up the logo for the company. It was like stopping a videotape and freeze-framing it to have a closer look at a character you've taken for granted.

I realised, first of all, that Piggley wasn't a baby piglet any more. I saw him now as the chief storyteller, the one who was making up all the personalised books. If he was a storyteller, he'd have to be more grown-up, with clothes to match. I gave him a dicky bow and a little waistcoat. Then I decided the waistcoat looked too formal, so I asked the artist to draw it in a check fabric, so Piggley would look like he came from the country. The painter, based on my descriptions, came up with the first drawings of Piggley Pooh and for the first time, my childhood friend began to figure in my adult life.

I had my baby in the August of that year. A little girl. Klaragh. I had been very decisive about the birth: I did not want Francis there. I had read somewhere in some magazine that if your husband was present at the childbirth he would go off you from a relationship point of view. When I read it, it made sense to me. You don't want your husband seeing you from that angle and it probably would put him off you. Francis didn't disagree with me, either. In fact he was slightly relieved. But then as the time approached, and it being our first baby, we had two or three false alarms. When I finally went into labour for real, I suddenly decided 'to hell with it, even if he goes off me, I want him here throughout this' and I insisted that he came in. He had done no research, attended no classes, assisted in no breathing, timed no contractions. He was totally ignorant and had not a clue as to what was going to happen. He knew the outline of it but none of the detail.

'I found it terribly shocking,' he remembers. 'Because my daughter was very dark black when she came out. Her whole body. She was very different to the children who were born to us later. She had a tough birth because it was the first and she was quite battered and bruised. I just couldn't believe the colour of her. She went pink after two minutes but I was totally gobsmacked.'

He may have felt totally gobsmacked, but he was very useful in that he was helping me get through the pain, and was giving me the emotional support I needed. It was the greatest moment of our lives to hold this new creation.

'It was a sea of emotion,' is how Francis sums it up. 'Wonderful once Klaragh turned pink and she was healthy. Then we could be happy. That was a great moment.'

There weren't many of those wonderful peaceful lazy moments of satisfaction after we took Klaragh home to our borrowed house. Too much was going on: we were trying to get planning permission to build a house and I was trying to build up my business. We were coming into our first Christmas in Stephen's Green and the books were flying off the shelves. The business was doing really well. Piggley Pooh was represented at the front of our 'premises' in the Stephen's Green Centre by a big stand-up cardboard cut-out, almost lifesize, and he attracted even more business to our small corner.

We had no idea that the same dicky-bowed storytelling pig was about to turn our lives inside out.

Chapter Eight

AND PIGS MIGHT FLY

Never mind Piggley Pooh's stories: at this point in our own story, we were married, we had a beautiful baby, Francis' legal practice was going well, we had a healthy franchise business and we now even had a pig, beautifully drawn by Ray Sherlock. Because the pig was getting a hold on the attention of the nation, Francis made sure we were legally protected and trademarked. I'd have felt silly trademarking a pig, but not so with Francis, who was convinced that this was a special pig with a big future. Trademarking him was a serious issue for Francis.

It was strange, for me, to see my childhood companion not just realised in a lovely cardboard cut-out, but registered in law, because up to that point I had never revealed Piggley Pooh to anyone other than to my brothers and sisters when we played together as children. But since I was older than they were, they don't really remember him. Later, when the Disney corporation suggested we had stolen his name from books about Winnie the Pooh available in Meath when I was growing up, I wished I had made more of an issue about Piggley with my brothers and sisters when they were children, because it would have allowed them to testify in court for me.

That major trouble was way in the future, however. After *Live at Three*, we had twenty-six titles in our personalised book range which – as soon as we changed the name to Piggley Pooh – became collectively known to the general public as 'The Piggley Pooh Books' although none of them actually featured a pig. One of them featured a farmyard story but it had a pig called Piggy or Porky. Piggley Pooh was a corporate, rather than a literary, reality at that point. We were trading using the name Piggley Pooh unhindered, unencumbered, unfettered for 1996. That was at least three years before Disney issued their first writ against us.

Because we were doing so well in Stephen's Green, we considered extending the franchise all over the country. Our vision was to create a version of The Body Shop or The Sock Shop: a retail franchise where the same excellent product is available on the same terms and to the same standards no matter where, geographically, the franchise happens to be located.

We eventually opened five retail franchises, bringing Piggley Pooh branches right around the country. We had three in Dublin, one in Limerick and one in Clare. All doing well. The people operating these franchises would order one hundred books and we would supply them from our stables in Meath. It nearly killed Francis because it was physical stuff. He would do 'the day job' in the law practice and then come home to a night of lifting boxes filled with books to service these franchises.

Francis had an assistant in the practice, Niall Sheerin, and even Niall got roped in. When some emergency happened, he would be asked to go and serve in a Piggley Pooh store.

'He was a law graduate like myself,' Francis recalls. 'So for peers of ours to see us hauling these boxes and serving these books was a tremendous kick. They slagged us constantly: "Don't tell me you spent years going to law school and college to flog books about teddy bears and pigs."'

Behind all of the jeering, however, was a realisation that our trademarked logo figure had an odd appeal. One of Francis' legal friends told him about an American client who chanced on the Stephen's Green Piggley Pooh store and said to him in passing: 'that Piggley Pooh would be a brilliant television character.'

That legal friend, Robert Ryan, who still acts for us as our lawyer, also knew someone in an animation company called Terraglyff run by two guys named Gerry Sheerin and Russell Boland.

'Look, why don't you meet these guys,' Robert said to Francis. 'Why don't you meet them and see if they're interested in taking over the pig and making him into an animated character? Even if they're not interested, they're nice guys and you could get some useful advice from them about making the most of Piggley Pooh.'

Francis met with them in the spring of 1996. These two men had worked for major studios like Warner Brothers and Disney and Spielberg. They had come out of Sullivan Bluth, which was a major player in the animation industry in Dublin ten years previously, and were now creating video games. They thought Piggley Pooh had potential, but they were also realistic about the business of animation and its miseries.

'We can't tell you whether it's going to be a success or not,' one of them told Francis. 'We agree that it's very interesting.'

'But you could go and spend £100m,' the other added. 'Which you won't be able to raise anyway and it could be a disaster or you could strike it lucky. Chances of you striking it lucky are maybe one in a million – maybe one in ten million.'

'But unless you do it,' said the first, 'You will never know.'

Of course those are the fatal words to Francis and me. We *wanted* to know. We were born to take risks. Each in our different way. I get nervous in the face of a challenge but I never panic and I am fundamentally convinced that any individual can do anything, if they put their mind to it. In the years that followed, Francis and I often found ourselves doing worst-scenario planning. One of us would notice the other looking desolate.

'OK, what's the worst that can happen?' I'd say. 'That we have to sell up here and go to America, to start off again? We can do that.'

Or Francis would say: 'Listen, Denise, if things get bad enough, we can go to Australia. Start over.'

We never gambled gratuitously. But fail to take a chance? Forget it. We always felt we had to take those risks. So when these two men sketched out the risks for Francis, he gestured the downside away and wanted to know how to progress the idea further. Immediately. They suggested that we contact a small studio where they could do a mock-up pilot for us.

We contacted Brown Bag, a tiny studio in Gardiner Street in a run-down area in Dublin. Just four years later, Brown Bag were to get an Oscar nomination for *Give Up Your Oul Sins*. But that was in the future. In 1996, three people sat down in an office that you could barely call an office in an impoverished area of Dublin, one of them being Francis Fitzpatrick, and decided to make a short animated film to promote the possibilities of a Piggley Pooh series. The other two, Cathal Gaffney and Darragh O'Connell, were miles ahead of Francis, at that point, in their knowledge of the business.

'Why don't you apply for a grant from the European Commission?' they asked.

Francis wrote down the details of applying for an EU grant.

'Oh, and there's a cartoon forum every year,' they added. 'That's where the European Commission pump about £5m into new animations. As a venue, the European Commission always pick a disadvantaged rural area. The forum has been in places recently like Turkey and Finland. But this year, 1996, it's heading for Connemara in Galway.'

Francis quickly digested the fact that the Eurovision of

cartoons was due to take place in the west of Ireland that very year and realised that any serious contenders for the huge money involved had better be there with some promising product samples. Brown Bag already had their own project but they were happy to be guns for hire. However, that meant that Francis was going to have to finance whatever product he was going to make around Piggley Pooh. Francis agreed with the guys from Brown Bag that Piggley Pooh could be one of the four projects out of Ireland produced for the event.

He then set about putting together a hundred promotional booklets. For speed, he put his own name on the brochure. When I discovered it, I went berserk.

'There was only room for one name as the creator and the people doing the brochure, because they'd met me, they naturally thought –' Francis began.

I didn't let one more syllable come out of him. I yelled at him that he was stealing my stories, my character, robbing me of part of my childhood. It felt as if he was snatching my birthright away from me.

'I don't understand why you're mad,' Francis said to me, flummoxed. 'We're a team. We're husband and wife. We're the same. It doesn't matter if your name is on it or my name is on it.'

'It bloody well *does* matter,' I hissed.

'But it's just words on a bit of paper, why should it matter so much?'

I couldn't explain to him how outraged I felt. I could not align the notion of teamwork and partnership and me as the originator with the fact that he was the one whose name was on the paperwork. I couldn't do anything, even throw a meaningful dramatic tantrum. I marched out of the room and, banging the door behind me, went upstairs into the bedroom and threw myself on the bed where he could see me. But he

107

didn't follow me upstairs so that was wasted. In retrospect, it's mildly funny, but at the time it was deeply wounding. I was lying there crying, feeling absolutely betrayed – and, worst of all, betrayed by Francis. It was the first time and I felt out of control. That I had let the brochure get this far without looking at it. That I had trusted him and now he had gone and done the dirt on me.

What maddened me most was his lack of understanding. He was genuinely surprised that I would think that he would do all this work and not get any recognition. The way he saw it there was no problem with him being chief executive (or whatever the title was on the brochure) because he was doing as much as I was doing. But my outlook was that he had his law career and that this – Piggley Pooh – was mine. He was helping me with this like I was helping him with his law. (I used to assist him with the book-keeping involved in his practice.)

While I was wasting my time flopping on the bed without him being there to witness it, Francis was having a nervous breakdown trying to photocopy and collate half a million pages. He worked solidly through ten hours because he had to meet a deadline the following morning.

Normally, I'd have helped him, but hell was going to freeze over before I would help him after what he'd done to me, so he had to work for hours loading paper, unwrapping bundles of paper, slamming down the binder, all with a ferocious pain in his back and a matching one in his head after the row with me. So both of us remember that battle with horror, as a gruesome blip in our normal pattern.

We're fortunate that we're complementary personalities. If he had to, Francis could remember every detail of a slight or an offence and stay not speaking to someone for years over that slight or offence. I'm quite different. I can sulk for maybe eight hours if I really try, but even that is pushing it.

I actually forget what a row has been about, if I have to leave the resolution of it over night. Whenever I have a fight, I have to deal with it that day, not because of the old thing of 'not letting the sun go down on your wrath' but because if I slept on it, I would wake up the following morning having completely forgotten I was having a row with someone or what the subject of the row was.

When I sleep on things at night I can resolve them in my unconsciousness so that the next morning what was a major issue the night before has gone away, evaporated. This episode was probably the worst disagreement we ever had with each other. (We had plenty of disagreements with external individuals and corporations later, but we met them with a united front.) It hurt us both deeply, because each side was as convinced as the other that their position was justified, that the other person was being grossly unfair and self-indulgent and that personal dignity demand that each stand up and be counted.

But we got over it. We had to because out of the blue, we were shifting businesses, moving into animated movies and away from publishing. (We were, of course, planning to stay in publishing as well as making films.) We were moving into animation knowing no more about it than we had known about publishing when we got started on the personalised books. It would have been frightening, except that it was happening at too fast a pace.

In my case, I was watching a little secret character come out from the back of my head, where he'd lived since I was a toddler, and start to become 'A Property' and 'A Character' with all sorts of people discussing his traits, characteristics and wardrobe and asking me to elaborate on stories involving him or being told by him. Deciding that he should have a check waistcoat suddenly seemed a very simple decision.

We were meeting fascinating people and we were in a

totally exciting industry. It was and is an industry that captivates people who do not comprehend the details of what is involved at all. Francis and I noticed that when we'd be at a party, talking in company, and the subject of Piggley Pooh's progress would come up, we'd mention animation and people would say 'animation?' They mightn't know what you were talking about but they were interested. It's one of those intriguing words.

The personalised book business was still vitally important to us and, as a businesswoman, I was determined that while we could – and would – have a lot of fun developing Piggley Pooh from the back of my head into a big primary-coloured animated cartoon on screen, until we broke into some kind of big time, we needed to keep the franchise ticking over profitably. I employed a girl called Suzanne Taite in the June of that year who worked out wonderfully and took the pressure off me. Suzanne is still with us after all these years and has been a great support and friend. We still had our shop front and were planning that it would be a venue for any further merchandise, if we went down the animation road.

Piggley Pooh stories – innocent stories – began to build into scripts. Piggley Pooh was the ringleader with a sidekick named Churchill, who was a Dalmatian. There was also Henrietta Hen who lived in the wheelbarrow. Each episode would set out an adventure. The friends would have to try and sort something out in the farmyard. Nothing worked on the farm by electrical or diesel power. It was all done manually because it wasn't based on the real-life operation of a farm, viewed from the point of view of the farmer, but on the kind of antics that we'd get up to as toddlers, like going down to collect pinkeens.

Half-recalled memories. Innocent, playful stories. A world of activity but no evil; complications but no cares. In addition, there was a link back to the oldest tradition of storytelling for children: stories with a moral twist to them. Not a major moral twist, just a line or two at the end of a story where, say, some of the characters cheated, which would remind the young viewers that cheating does nobody any good. As we moved the project along, it seemed to be important that there be something in each episode from which children could learn, because at the time education was losing traction with younger children and the easiest 'sell' for any cartoon was to have lots of violence, brutality, fire, flame and action heroes.

Let's be clear. Cartoons have always been violent. Whenever we went to the cinema as children, I always loved *Tom and Jerry*. The cartoons involving the two of them were extremely violent, but it was improbable funny violence, and very little of that kind of harmless outrageous cartoon material was being made for children when we were getting started on Piggley Pooh. The world of cartoons was a harsh one. I just wanted not so much to tell particular stories as to let today's children sample the innocence and pleasure of my own childhood on the farm.

My hero, Piggley, was a great *seanchaí*. The seanchaí was one of the unifying figures in communities all around Ireland for generations. Long before television or radio an old man or woman in the neighbourhood would remember and recount stories. Those stories might be embellished accounts of local events or elaborate renditions of great sagas or legends. While, in summertime, there might be dancing at the crossroads, in wintertime, the seanchaí was the main entertainment. Families would gather around the open fire and listen to the storyteller.

I saw Piggley as being that kind of figure, recounting the events of his life, telling the stories of when he was young. You'd see the old Piggley and the younger Piggley. You'd see the love story between Pigaleen and Piggley Pooh.

I also envisaged a theme partly based on the practice common among the ancient kings of Ireland of fostering out their children to other families, but even more resonant of the recurring motif (in the Irish oral tradition and in fairy stories the world over) of the 'changeling', a fairy who is substituted for the real child in the cradle, with the real child being spirited away. I imagined Piggley being convinced that he was of royal blood and had been switched at birth. But, because Piggley was going to be a seanchaí, he would also have the opportunity to tell simple versions of the Celtic legends that go back into pre-history.

While I was playing with script ideas, Francis was working on finance. He managed to clear the first hurdle by getting the EU European Commission grant of £24k. Effectively it was only £12k, because when they say the grant is £24k you've got to match equity so each side puts in £12k. That was a hell of a lot of money at the time when we didn't have a hell of a lot of money. Brown Bag were delighted because it meant that they were going to work on a properly funded project: the £24k went to them and they had work for the summer.

At the end of the summer, we owned a pilot three-minute animated film, which for its time was extremely good. £24k doesn't get you anything close to what $24m does but if you look back it was as good as anyone else was doing at the time. Our little pilot meant we were going down to Connemara as the home champions.

Much bigger TV production houses were going to be there, showing lengthier and more sophisticated pilot materials, but what they lacked was the absolute drive, commitment and verve that we had. I wasn't sitting on the sidelines, acknowledging that I knew nothing about animation and deferring to all the experts. I was demanding that we win this competition, no matter what we had to do to win it.

'What about my law practice?' Francis asked plaintively at one stage, when it looked as if Piggley Pooh had taken over every aspect of our lives.

'To hell with your law practice,' I told him eagerly. 'This will take us much further than your practice ever will!'

He looked at me with an expression of mixed doubt and delight. On the one hand, he was listening to the certainties of a woman with neither knowledge nor experience of the area she was so sure about. On the other, animation, film-making and TV production were a lot more interesting than the standard work he could expect to encounter in a small legal practice. He was determined to continue to service the practice though and did so through an assistant, through mobile phones and through turning up at meetings when he needed to. But his main focus was on the Piggley Pooh project.

Within that project, the fact that he was a lawyer was an enormous help. It meant he was able to walk into KPMG Corporate Finance, who have a track record of funding films made in Ireland in the last decade or so, and work with Mary Leonard, who was the guru at the time. Not that Mary was exactly encouraging in the early days: 'Listen, you have no chance in hell, Francis,' she said. 'I'm going to tell you straight here and now, this is going to be a disaster. I'm going to wish you the very best of luck but on average it's not even a ten million to one shot. It's beyond that.'

'Mary, thank you very much for your frankness,' Francis said, knowing she expected him to walk out of her office with his metaphorical tail between his real legs. 'But now will you be part of the team because we need to do business?'

She looked at his beaming enthusiastic face and sighed that particular sigh that means 'Uh, oh. This one's a sl-o-o-o-w learner'.

'I need you to realise you're not going to make any money

out of this,' she told him. 'Go back to your law practice.'

'I commend you for that very good advice,' Francis said, not skipping a beat. 'Now, will you be part of the team?'

Even though Mary Leonard joined us in a kind of baffled way – recognising that Francis had listened to her good, if negative advice, and then ignored it – she then got totally behind us, as did her team from KPMG. Consequently, moving *en masse* with one short pilot down to the Connemara festival, we took with us a team of suited guys and girls: KPMG, lawyers, accountants and a friend of Francis who works for BT in London, Manoj Chawla.

I wore the best outfits I owned so that I'd look business-like but not dull. As far as Francis was concerned, we were on a major marketing expedition. We had to sell, sell, sell. I wasn't that sure what we were selling to who, but felt it would be good if we could get a buzz going around Piggley Pooh.

It was pretty clear, within a few hours of our arrival, that the buzz was already underway and that all we had to do was increase its volume a bit. Somehow, word had spread that we were being funded by an American christian broadcasting authority. Someone seemed to have dreamed up this scenario because no one could explain how we had appeared out of nowhere with a credible pilot. Moving as quickly as we had meant that rumours hadn't even had a chance to build up around us, so as far as the majority of people at the Connemara venue were concerned, we had materialised out of nothing. It wasn't just that we were unknown on the international front: no one had ever heard of us in Ireland. Yet we were making huge waves. So there had to be an explanation and someone duly provided it. Never mind the reality, the conspiracy theory was great!

It helped that a friend of mine in Smurfit Publications named Sandra Sheridan mentioned to me in advance of Connemara that they print *Cara* magazine, the complimentary magazine tucked into the seat-pocket on every Aer Lingus flight coming into the country.

Cara is a high-quality glossy which many passengers, having glanced over it, tend to take away with them when they disembark. Sandra was able to put me in touch with Vince Devaux who was the editor.

'I need some publicity in *Cara*,' I told him. 'It has to be *Cara*, because Aer Lingus is the airline of choice for the people coming over from Brussels.'

Francis and I were just hoping that, as editor, Vince would 'do the decent' by us and slip in a mention. In fact, what he generously did went so far beyond decency, it nearly got us fired from the competition. What he did was run a feature on the cartoon forum, illustrated by its logo. Marginally altered. He had his artists change the cartoon forum logo and put the Piggley Pooh logo instead of it. This was magnificent for us because everyone on the plane learned *only* about Piggley Pooh, one character in one production out of eighty contestants.

Cara was one element to the buzz surrounding Piggley Pooh which was already well-established in the first few hours at Connemara. Another contributor to that buzz was the fact that Cathal Gaffney from Brown Bag had been able to get Piggley Pooh on the Dave Fanning film show. A small ten-second piece was aired. It was enough to make us hot favourites. One half of me was delighted by this. The other half wondered if being the favoured contender could be a disadvantage. All the time, we were trying to play it cool in a situation which was becoming positively surreal.

When we arrived in Connemara, we were greeted by two of the stalwarts of Irish animation: Aidan Hickey and Eamon Lawless. Eamon Lawless is head of Fred Wolf Films, one of the major world producers which, among other projects, animated *Budgie the Helicopter* for Sarah Ferguson, Duchess of

York. Aidan Hickey is a scriptwriter and he's been in the business for thirty years. They are the best known names in the business – together with Jimmy Murakami who was also there – and all the guys in the studios pay homage to them.

Yet on this occasion, when we went to say hello to them, they didn't even answer. They totally blanked us. Cut us dead. Aidan Hickey didn't *say* 'Get out of my face' but he made his rage so obvious that Francis felt he should go and greet him again and see what was going on. When he went over, Hickey turned his back on Francis and walked silently away.

Francis was standing there, unable to understand what was happening, when somebody from Brussels with whom he had been very friendly in a number of earlier encounters came over to where he was. Yolanda was her name and she was in charge of the event. It quickly became obvious that any positive relationship from the past was not so much history as pre history. She was livid with Francis.

'I was trying to understand why Aidan Hickey was cutting me dead,' Francis remembers. 'And before I could get a handle on *that*, I find myself face to face with Yolanda, who the last time we'd talked was in great humour, and now, *she's* enraged with me. I just had no idea what I had done.'

'You've cheated,' Yolanda told him. 'You're barred from the competition.'

'How could I have cheated?'

'You advertised instead of the European Commission on the Aer Lingus brochure,' was the response. 'You're out. We've moved to bar you and your team from the competition.'

She stalked off in a fury, leaving Francis confused and scared – but not guilty, because none of us had set out to break any rules we knew about. All of us gathered together as a team.

'What's wrong? What have we done? Why's everybody mad at us?'

Francis explained. A long silence ensued, as we all absorbed the information and its grim implications.

'What are we going to do?' I asked.

I could sense people looking at me and wondering, although not wondering aloud, why I was being so dense. There was nothing we *could* do except slink home. But I knew that however fazed Francis might be by what had happened, he would not be in slink-home mode, any more than I was.

'We've come this far and we've nothing to lose,' he said, quietly. 'I'm going to play the injunction card.'

We all agreed this would be a good move, mainly because none of us could think of another move to substitute for it. Francis went off to seek out Yolanda and get her into a quiet corner.

'The competition isn't going ahead,' he told her.

'What are you talking about? Of course it is. You're just not going to be in it.'

'I'm making an application to the high court in Galway tomorrow morning before the competition starts and I'm going to seek an injunction against you.'

'You can't do that.'

'Oh yes I can and I have my legal team ready to go.'

A flurry of activity broke out while Francis and I had coffee with our team and tried to give the impression that we had the whole problem legally sewn up. Then the head of the whole animation sector in Europe came over to Francis and pulled him aside for a quiet word.

'What you've done is absolutely disgraceful,' she told him icily. 'However, we cannot afford for the competition not to go ahead. So you are being readmitted. Be very clear, though: any more transgressions and you're out.'

Francis nodded gravely and walked back to his group

indicating by his expression that none of us was to leap up and down or fist the air with delight.

'I was really gambling,' he told us. 'There is no way a judge would have issued a writ suspending the competition. Damages would have been an adequate recompense so I was just chancing my arm but I had to do it.'

'It's worked, let's get on with it,' I said, hugely relieved.

Neither of us let on to be weak with relief, but we both were. Each of us knew we hadn't enough money to go further and that failure to proceed would have left us in a deep financial hole. Losing money would have been bad. Losing the public position we had created would have been worse. We had arrived in Connemara as leaders, Francis having almost completely sidelined his lucrative legal practice. Had we been removed from the competition, all of our creative work, all of the time commitment, all of the finance we had scraped together, would have been irrevocably lost. Nobody in animation would ever take us seriously again, and a cloud would hang over Francis' judgement for having sunk so much time and brain power into something and then wrecking it at the last minute because of apparently persuading or provoking *Cara* magazine to do what they did with the logo.

We presented the character. Positive reaction immediately emerged. Interest was expressed by major broadcasters including the BBC and TFI from France.

It had been a rocky few days, but it now looked as if my brain child, Piggley Pooh, might be moving onto the screen and destined for a starring role.

Chapter Nine

'NO BUY!' AT THE CANNES TELEVISION FESTIVAL

It was like a mad game of Snakes and Ladders. Having slid down the snake of the logo controversy, we climbed back up the ladder of Big Broadcaster approval. The next ladder led to the Cannes Television Festival, known to the TV world as 'MIPCOM'.

We had believed, all along, that one of the best potential markets for Piggley Pooh was the vast, or at least potentially vast, American market, characterised by millions of parents and grandparents who would have a direct or inherited nostalgia for an innocent rural Ireland. In many ways, although Ireland was an early member of what was then the European Economic Community, now the European Union, the link with America was tremendously strong. The US is home to seventy million Irish Americans. We believed that this had to be our prime audience. Television tends to work that way: America is the big market and all others are ancillary. The European Union was going to be important, but secondary to our aims.

Francis was convinced that he could sell to America and fished around until he learned that the key place to be, if you wanted to get your product in front of US viewers, was the Cannes Television Festival in the autumn. So Cannes it was going to be, as we moved through the summer of 1997. At this stage, we had been married three years and were making roughly £30k a year between Francis' law work and the Piggley Pooh books, so we were thrilled to be going to Cannes: the forum for all television that is sold worldwide.

What we did not know at that time was that Cannes is for people who have television series made. People who have their productions complete, edited, ready to broadcast. Cannes is where you sell product, not ideas. It's a TV/film supermarket. Which meant that the Fitzpatricks, with their cute little pilot and their brochures, were like someone standing in the aisle of a supermarket trying to interest customers in the *idea* of a new kind of jam.

It was the wrong forum but the two of us set off in optimistic ignorance. We stayed outside Cannes and hired the smallest, cheapest car we could lay our hands on. I would drive Francis to the Palais des Festival (the conference centre in Cannes) every morning, all fresh-faced and crisp in his business suit, carrying his neat briefcase with three or four promotional tapes and some pictures of Piggley Pooh. By the time I would pick him up in the evening, it was as if he had been fed through a woodchopper. He would be dishevelled, crumpled, barely capable of speech and with his tie missing. The Before and After shots would provide a perfect visual summary of what Cannes is like.

Going in, on the first day, Francis could have been a Martian, it was all so strange to him. He had no idea if there were any other Irish people present. (There were, but he discovered that only after three days.) Imagine the rugby grounds at Lansdowne Road fully enclosed. Now, insert into that vast space hundreds of television stations, each with its own 12 x 4 stand, each manned by salespeople frantically trying to sell television programming to executives from other countries.

It's high-powered, high-pressure stuff, and the last thing any of them want is some Irish greenhorn coming up to them and saying: 'I've got a pig with a check waistcoat.' Francis was lucky to get out of there alive at the end of each day. He was investing energy, determination and wild hope into ramming a huge square peg into a vast round hole. It never struck either of us, each day as I dropped him off, filled with hope, that we might be in the wrong place at the wrong time. Looking back, we couldn't have been in a wronger place at a worse time, us with our huge ambitions and matching lack of knowledge.

Even if we had been in the *right* place, we'd have been like tourists dropped in the middle of Athens without a map. You can't buy a textbook at the entrance to the Cannes Television Festival which tells you to do x if you want to achieve y. They just give you a huge bible which tells you where each exhibit is, but it would take you five or six hours just to get to grips with the publication, never mind get any work done.

A lot of people at the exhibition don't speak English although it's officially the main language of the festival. Because of his own linguistic background, Francis is one of the few men I know who realises, in a very practical way, that English is only the third largest language in the world. First there's Mandarin and then there's Spanish. About the only advantage Francis had, at that first visit to Cannes, was a little bit of Mandarin.

Francis stood at the entrance to an exhibition centre which seemed to be half the size of the world. He had convinced himself before he ever started that America was no problem because of all the Irish in America so – in his own mind – that market was done and dusted, he had already conquered it. This gave him an advantage, albeit built on sand, since anyone going into Cannes who has conquered America will find it easier to sell their product because everyone in the world wants to buy American programming.

'I just have to talk to people as if I have America conquered,' Francis told himself, and went looking for Japanese stands, since Japan is the second biggest market after the US.

He threaded his way along the aisles, being shoulder-jostled by crowds of pressured visitors. Music, sound effects and commentary in a dozen languages spewed from the displays on either side of the walking areas. It felt like New York at night. Making his way to Tokyo Broadcasting's display, Francis spotted that the people working on the stand were scanning the crowds with knowing eyes.

'The Japanese guys see me coming and they know I'm a timewaster. I can see them knowing that I'm a timewaster. It was horrendous. So I go over and I say "Hello, I'm from Ireland." They don't speak any English but they do speak enough to say "No buy!" I said "But I've something for you —" "NO BUY!" they're shouting at me in front of everybody. If you had any dignity at all, you'd curl and shrivel and die. Thankfully I didn't. So I kept persisting. "No, no buy," one big Japanese sumo wrestler type said to me. "Go away."'

Lest Francis misunderstand the instruction, the big Japanese guy pushed him out of the way and off the raised section of the stand back onto the floor of the exhibition centre. Time to re-group, Francis thought. He walked away, face burning with the humiliation, looking for somewhere to sit down, thinking 'Christ, I'm in the middle of a different world here. This is a world market. I know no one, I don't know what to do. I'll just give up and wait till Denise collects me. Go over to the pub.'

Before heading to the pub, he sat down and got himself a cup of coffee. As the caffeine seeped into his veins, determination seeped back into him, too.

'I've paid my money to be here,' he said to himself. 'Why not give it a go?'

The disqualifying phrase 'No buy!' rattled around in his head and – like the good salesman he is – he tried to look at the encounter from the other man's point of view.

'Maybe he's selling something,' Francis thought. 'Yes,

that's it. If he's not buying maybe he's selling. So that's where I need to begin. I'll give it one last go.'

Putting down the coffee cup, Francis headed right back to the Toyko TV stand. The big sumo wrestler saw him returning and was visibly irritated. Other staff at the stand began to fend Francis off, trying to explain to him that he was getting in the way, stopping them doing their job, selling their programmes. The sumo wrestler decided they were wasting time telling Francis he was wasting time, and he let a roar out of him, smacking his two big meaty hands down on the surface in front of him so that brochures and leaflets flipped over from the wind created.

'NO BUY!' he shouted.

Francis shouted back at him: 'I buy!' he bellowed.

Within thirty seconds, he was sitting among new friends, drinking saki. The entire relationship was transformed. The exhibitors were showing him catalogues. One of them found an English translator so they could interrogate this particular buyer from Ireland. The interrogation went like this:

'How big is your company?'

'Biggest of its kind in Ireland.'

True, but Francis is talking about a small unique franchise making personalised books, whereas the interrogator assumes he's talking about a vast broadcasting operation.

'How many branches do you have?'

'We've five at the last count but we're only new.'

Again, quite true, but not strictly relevant.

They went into a little huddle to consider what they were learning.

'No one in Europe rates Japanese animation,' Francis offered, getting expansive on the strength of the saki. 'Nobody has copped on that, when it's going to be big, it's going to be so big. No European buyer has spotted the potential I see here. I'm telling you here and now.'

Francis may have thought he was bullshitting but, as events turned out, he was absolutely bang on about the potential of Japanese animation. If he had stopped at that point, listened to what he was saying and decided to act as a broker bringing Japanese animation to the European market, he would have found Pokémon. Pokémon happened two years later. Francis, as I often remind him, would have been one of the first in and would have made his millions without having any battle with the Disney corporation.

At the time, however, Francis was not going to get distracted. He was too intent on creating a relationship with these men which would allow him, in due course, to sell them our pig. He started name-dropping. Shamelessly claiming he knew Kevin Lenihan on children's television in RTÉ, that he knew Kevin Dawson. One name after another poured out. He could have said Paddy Mac and they would have said 'Ah yes, please introduce us.'

'I'll take all your stuff and show it to my contacts,' Francis said eventually, 'But you've got to take my brochure and find out if someone will buy my pig.'

'Ah yes,' they said, giving the brochure a cursory glance. 'Very interesting, nice pig.'

That afternoon, when I collected Francis, he still had the woodchopper-victim look to him, but was much more upbeat, albeit also more realistic.

'I can sell here,' he said. 'But you have to have your offering so well packaged. We're here with the wrong packaging and presentation. But I'm still glad we came, still glad to be here. It's a beginning.'

We went out to dinner that night and had a good night. In the next couple of days Francis encountered other Europeans and Irish people, who were startled to run into him and puzzled by what a lawyer was doing in Cannes, where he seemed to be something of a misfit.

'They were helpful,' he remembers gratefully. 'They told me what the market was all about.'

For the first time, on the third day, Francis came to the realisation that he was actually part of the European independents group which, if he'd known on the first day, would have been very helpful because it's actually quite a large grouping of independents and they have a lot of facilities you can use. When Francis eventually found his way to their area on the top floor he learned that there was quite a lot of support and that he wasn't as alone as he had imagined.

On the other hand, the support being offered was predicated on the assumption that you had a TV programme made and ready to sell. It was not designed for and could be of no use to someone who had an idea based on a country girl's memories of her childhood. They gently explained that, at Cannes, you can't really do anything with an idea and a promo unless you're extremely lucky.

'The chances are you're not going to be that lucky,' one of the Irish contingent told him. 'Because we can't even sell programming, never mind make a programme from scratch.'

Francis listened gratefully and made notes of their advice. But, at the same time, he knew he couldn't afford to believe them. Not in the sense of them not telling the truth. Of course they were telling the truth. He just couldn't afford to have that truth apply to our product.

'Their views of the horizon were very narrow,' he remembers. '"Irish programmes can't be sold internationally," they kept saying, "no one ever buys them." I couldn't listen to this. I had to sell to America. In my own mind I was certain I would sell to America. Never mind the standard experience. Never mind that I should have programmes made. Never mind the reality, I was going to sell to America, and then the world, starting at Cannes.'

Some of his new-found mentors told Francis about an

agent named Len Giarruputo. Francis wrote down the name and the stand number – he thinks it was stand 3, point 17. First thing the following morning, when he was fresh and un-mulched, he set off to find it. The agent was there when he arrived. A man in his early seventies, steeped in television, cynical in the face of salesmanship.

'Hi Len,' Francis said, breezing up, all business. 'I've got a terrific programme for the US market.'

Len raised an interrogative eyebrow.

'Programme? How many episodes? What's the genre? What's the target audience?'

'Did I say "programme"?' Francis responded. 'I actually meant a pilot.'

Len settled back down, like a lion who'd thought a sheep was on the menu and was now learning no more than a lamb chop was on offer.

'That's no good,' he growled. 'Come back to me when you've got a programme made.'

'Well, I need $7m to make the programme,' Francis pointed out. 'And I can't make the programme without getting someone to buy it.'

'Hold on sonny boy,' Len said. 'You can't sell a pilot here. This is Cannes. This is where programmes that are made are sold.'

'And if you can't sell it in Cannes, you can't sell it anywhere,' Francis added, trying to keep the conversation going, but unclear as to where he could take it next.

'You're right there, sonny.'

Francis stood there, willing Len to find him interesting. Len, with decades of experience under his belt, must, watching Francis, have realised that while this young guy clearly didn't know what he was doing, he wasn't easy to squash, wasn't easy to get rid of. Perhaps because he's an agent, and so must always be invested in possibility and in trace ele-

126

ments of potential, Len didn't concentrate on Francis being a neophyte. Instead, what he registered was an intoxicating mix because Francis was a lawyer who was very articulate, very driven and who was now spouting facts and figures about the American population and the proportion of the overall population who acknowledged that they were of Irish origin.

With an air of sacrificing good commercial time, he looked at the demo DVD and examined the brochures. He then asked questions about the kind of stories Piggley Pooh would tell in each episode of any potential series. To some of the questions, Francis knew the answers, whereas in a lot of cases, he was making it up as he went along, determined to get himself lodged in this man's mind.

'You could sell this to America,' Len eventually told Francis. 'I'll set up a couple of meetings, you pay me a percentage share of any sale. OK?'

'OK,' Francis said, and through Len, found himself booked to talk to WLIW 21, the fourth biggest station in the network of the Public Broadcasting Services in the US. Francis got a meeting with their buying agent, Tom Salmon.

It should not have happened. Not by the unwritten laws of Cannes, and certainly not according to the expectations of the much more experienced TV producers who had given Francis advice based on their track record. Francis was a young greenhorn, not even at the starting blocks of a TV production career. Len was an experienced man of the world, in the sunset years of a career, at precisely the point when he didn't need to take on any over-eager, under-informed, under-resourced youngsters from Ireland. As Francis remembers it, it was just a case of that magic, mutual 'click'.

'I took to him and him to me quite quickly. He could see that I had plenty of energy and nothing else. Subsequently talking to him, I asked him straight out why did he ever take me on. "I could see it in your eyes," he told me. "You were determined to make it happen. For me? OK, I was going to lose out on commission in terms of time I spent with you nursing you along, but that wasn't a huge loss, it was worth a shot.'"

While all of this was going on, I was on the beach. Cannes is a beautiful place. It's the greatest beach resort I've ever been at. I absolutely adore it. It's clean and the waves are nice and it's got all the facilities. You can have lunch on the beach, you can have drinks brought to you. It's beautiful. It's safe. It's a holiday resort the kings of England used to frequent. I loved it.

Juxtapose the picture of me on the beach in my bikini sipping a tall heavily iced drink complete with its own little parasol, and Francis lashing around an over-crowded hostile exhibition centre trying to flog the wrong product using the wrong format against a plethora of prophecies of doom, and you'd be forgiven for thinking this was cruel to Francis. In fact, although it looked as if it was taking years off his life, he would arrive out to be picked up each evening sodden, crumpled but unresentful of the darkening tan of his increasingly relaxed wife.

'I was made for Cannes,' is how he puts it, today. 'Cannes was my ultimate destination in life. When I go to Cannes now it's like going home. It was designed, dreamed up, built and operated for me. If there's such a thing as destiny, mine had to be Cannes. It's the most magnificent arena if you like people and if you can relate to people. If you can't, you've no business being there. It's a people place and it's a seller's place. I'd never have achieved the satisfaction that I've achieved in life if I hadn't been there.'

Last year, as Francis readied himself for another trip there, someone asked him to describe what Cannes is like for him, and he paraphrased Arnold Swartzenegger's words

Denise with her parents, Jimmy and Maura Swan

Francis with his father, Frank

Denise and Francis on their wedding day
Photograph courtesy of James Carney

Klaragh and Molly with Denise

Klaragh, Molly, Patrick, George and Daniel

Klaragh, George, Patrick and Daniel with
some Piggley Winks merchandise

The boys playing rugby
All photographs on this page by Seamus Farrelly

Klaragh with our dog, Jock

Daniel with our dogs, Jock and Jill

The whole family at the kitchen table

Denise and Francis at home
All photographs on this page by Seamus Farrelly

The baby, Molly, and Klaragh

Our house, Bramblewood
Both photographs by Seamus Farrelly

when he was invested with the seal of California as its elected governor: 'I came with nothing to Cannes, Cannes, you've given me everything.'

The agent said that we should go over to New York, because when you go to Cannes you can't meet people except by appointment. You might run into them in a bar or an elevator, but if you do, you have to condense all the subtleties of your programme into a two-sentence pitch. (Hence the phrase *Elevator Pitch*. That's all you've got: ten seconds to hit a bullseye.)

Three months later, we went to New York to meet first of all with Len, and then with Tom Salmon. Salmon listens to their sales pitch with a laugh bubbling under his serious expression, because he is amazed at the effrontery of both men. But he doesn't throw them out because, whatever about a kid from Ireland who doesn't know his animated arse from his elbow, Len is a wise old owl in TV terms. The question in Tom Salmon's head therefore is, why would Len take a chance with a kid who hasn't got a series made and has really no prospect of getting it made because where is he going to get $7m to make it with.

'How are you going to get the $7m?' Salmon asked Francis.

'I'm going to get it via a letter from you.'

'I'm not going to give you a letter saying I'm going to broadcast a series that's not been made, do you think I'm crazy?'

'No, you're not crazy. But you're a very nice man. Could you give me a letter that says if I raise the finance, you might?'

'I could do that.'

'That's all I need.'

Francis walked out of that TV station with a letter he decided would make our fortune. Now, the fact is that anyone of any intelligence who read that letter closely, would realise it was not worth the paper it was written on. There were so many non-specific possibilities and vaguely warm references that it didn't amount to anything when closely read. The whole game was to prevent anybody from reading it closely. Francis developed a patter around this issue that was sleight-of-hand set to music.

'For confidentiality reasons,' he'd say, sort of hesitating as if he was dying to let them read what was in his hand, 'I can't show you this other than, well, you could have a look, it's from PBS WLIW, the fourth biggest station in the nationwide PBS network in the US.'

At this point he would give them a brochure of WLIW but not the letter. The only time he let them see the letter, they would never get past the first paragraph, with its 'we were delighted to meet you' and 'you're very driven'. The whole performance reeked of enthusiasm that had to be kept under wraps for commercial reasons and, in theatrical terms, the letter was the core prop.

'It was enough to keep me going for the next two years,' Francis confirms. 'It got me in doors. People said "he may be new, but he's not totally off the wall here". I'm a lawyer, I present my lawyer's card. I present this extract from a document. I present a letter from the BBC letter we got after the Connemara showing, which says "Piggley Pooh is a fantastic character, we're very interested in him". But I do not show the subsequent letter from the BBC which says "we don't want him".'

By persuading people to put even their most grudgingly positive comments about our character on paper, Francis, unbeknownst to himself, was building up a portfolio giving the impression that Piggley Pooh was a serious player over which the transmitting networks of the world were competing.

Francis began to study the economics of film production

as if there was an exam coming up. The key question he had to answer was why a production company would take on the hassle of someone else's idea with the concomitant problem of finding $7m with which to make the programme, when they each had departments with their own ideas.

He knew, now, that he had to move my idea from a concept into something that could actually be product. Section 481/financing was the area of Irish tax legislation holding the most promise. Dreamed up as a way to reinforce Ireland's natural appeal to film-makers, it had attracted dozens of overseas film companies to come and make their feature films in the country. Neil Jordan made *Michael Collins* in Dublin, Spielberg made *Saving Private Ryan* in Wexford, and Mel Gibson became Braveheart in open Irish countryside with the help of half the Irish army as muscular extras.

Section 481 looks simple on the face of it. But it carries within itself a sting in the tail. In order to get ninety per cent of the budget from external investors, the main producer has to be capable of bringing ten per cent of the total to the table at the beginning. The ninety per cent is what will get the film made, but the first ten per cent is crucial to getting that overall enabling sum.

Francis had the ten per cent. Or at least a reasonably good prospect of raising it. Or as good a chance as could be created by a document from KPMG Corporate Finance which said that he was entitled, as an Irish citizen, to raise – tax free – ten per cent of the budget. In his mind, this meant that he already had that ten per cent, especially if prospective providers of the remaining ninety per cent didn't read the letter too closely. Once he pulled in that remaining ninety per cent of the budget, it would be no problem for him to stump up the last ten. It was just a problem of sequence, to be overcome by felicitous phrasing and a great deal of energetic hustling.

Neither of us was put off by the prospect of a little hustle, because we had learned that the television business is all about ideas and conviction. Even though, in theory, we should have been thrown out on our ear because we had no production to show, we were still in play: because we were so convinced of the value of our idea.

Piggley Pooh was gathering momentum because people loved it. There was an appetite for this kind of simple story-telling, this kind of innocence, not least because of a growing view that children's entertainment was too harsh and violent.

The feedback on Piggley was that this was different, this was fresh. This was what the industry needed. Because of that ready acceptance, hustling was fun, rather than an imposition. It's always easier to hustle on behalf of something you believe in. It's also easier to hustle hustlers. People in the film business are all hustlers. They have to be, because they never know the day nor the hour that their project will go belly-up because of some unforeseen circumstance, forcing them to turn to something else.

Every new executive that you meet has to justify their existence to their HQ or their investors. They're fearful that they'll go down in history as the ones who missed out on the Beatles or the purple dinosaur, so if they're approached about a new project – even if it's only a piddly little Piggley Pooh project – it's still a fresh idea and they will give time to checking it out.

Nor were we on our own. It's difficult, without this turning into an acknowledgments page, to mention all the people who give us that little boost, or invested time and money in our idea at one difficult point or another.

McConnells Advertising is a good example. Francis had a friend, Gareth Kinsella, who worked in that advertising agency and who became intrigued by our quest.

'We might be able to help you,' he said. (He didn't know what he was letting himself in for.)

'Manna from heaven,' Francis said. 'I'll take any help I can get, Gareth, I'm bleeding here, what can you do for me?'

'Come on in,' Gareth told him.

They looked at the idea, heard him recount his experiences in Cannes, our prospects with PBS and the constant drain on our finances that every step towards a TV series represented.

'Look, we're going to lose money on this,' the McConnells people said when they'd heard him out. 'But you never know, there might be something in it for us down the line. We have a new department starting which is kind of an ideas department and what we're prepared to do is to put together a full brochure for you and a full DVD presentation.'

'B-brilliant,' Francis stammered. 'What do I say – I mean, thank you.'

Without McConnells' generosity we could not have continued with the project nor played at the highest levels that we needed to. We will be forever grateful to them and in particular to Gareth and Pat Hurley. Francis and I wrote some material for a brochure about the character of Piggley Pooh, its background in my childhood on the farm and its fresh appeal to very young viewers.

McConnells took our stuff, edited it and designed a brochure around it. Its high production values made that brochure every bit as good as any brochure in Cannes. It did much more than try to flog a product. It set that product in a never-ending stream of Irish folklore going back to prehistory. It underlined how rich the Irish heritage, particularly in oral storytelling, is. It documented the breadth and depth of our national culture, reminding readers, as had Thomas Cahill in his bestseller *How the Irish Saved Civilisation*, that for centuries the Irish had educated the world through their missionaries, monasteries and illuminated manuscripts. Finally, it looked at the revival of confidence in Irish culture, talking about U2 and *Riverdance*.

That was the beginning of McConnells' generous and continuing contribution to the Piggley Pooh project. They became as convinced of its prospects as we were ourselves, and they never stinted. They continued to invest as much time and money without any idea of when – or if – they would get it back, or make any profit on the deal. We owe a real debt of gratitude to McConnells, without whose support and encouragement, we could not have succeeded.

A brochure doesn't sound as if it would make a huge difference, but it was one of a number of factors coming together that year which, together, created a momentum around the character and the project. Another apparently minor investment was made when Francis bought a tiny DVD player from Panasonic which put him miles ahead of the competition. Today, every second person has one of these little players, but this is five years ago, when they were rare.

Francis would arrive up to someone, introduce himself and explain that although he was a lawyer, he was involved in this fantastic animated film project. (The curiosity value of a lawyer being involved with a child's animation character had an odd way of attracting attention to the project.)

'Bottom line, I've got a brilliant television series from Ireland,' he would conclude.

'Yeah, but where is it?' would be the response of people unwilling to be dragged to some viewing booth somewhere. 'We can't see it.'

'Oh, yes you can,' Francis would say, producing the tiny player from behind his back and flipping it open so they could see the pilot.

He was playing it when he was buying drinks for people. He was playing it when he was in the elevator with prospects. He could play it walking along beside a viewer and hold it steady enough for them to be captivated. Which they always were.

One company based in Glasgow, named Cascade, were particularly interested. In December 1998, Francis met with them in Singapore at the Asian equivalent of the Cannes Television Festival. He met them again in New Orleans a few weeks later. By late spring, we had signed an option agreement with them. They would create an animated series based on our little pig and would sell it all over the world. Children who had never heard of Irish legends like the Salmon of Knowledge would be introduced to them through the storytelling of one small pig.

The director of Cascade, Ian Jones, was enormously optimistic about the future.

'I really look forward to working together on this project,' he wrote to us, 'and to help establish Piggley Pooh as a worldwide brand.'

Which sounded pretty good to Francis and me. Our little pig's dicky bow and waistcoat could become items as identifiable as Mickey Mouse's ears. It was just a matter of time. But maybe not that much time.

We knew, at this point, that we were on a winner with Piggley Pooh. We were getting deeper and deeper into debt, but that was OK. Creating a worldwide brand takes time and money. If we wanted Piggley to become a household name who would make us a fortune in the long term, we had to be prepared to invest in it in the short term. We had no problem with that. The future, for us and for our animated character, was filled with promise.

We reckoned without Disney.

Chapter Ten

THE MAGIC KINGDOM STRIKES BACK

The logo of the corporation set up by Walt Disney is easily identifiable. The founder's surname dominates. The name looks as if it's been sketched, freehand, and then a looping line placed beneath it. It's familiar, even to filmgoers who never watch the Disney channel on TV, because they have seen it so often at the beginning of feature-length animated movies, going back as far as *Snow White and the Seven Dwarfs* and *Fantasia*, and coming up as close to the present as *The Lion King* and *Pocahontas*. They automatically fill in the turrets of the Magic Kingdom behind the name, and you almost expect Tinkerbell to fly around dotting it with sparkles.

To us, the Disney logo carries very different connotations, all of them unpleasant. That started on the morning of 21 January 1999, when Francis, opening an envelope dropped by a courier, found a letter on official Disney letterhead. It was a Notice of Opposition letter from Frank B. Dehn and Associates in London, the European trademark agents for Disney. It had been forwarded to us by our own trademark agents, McLachlan & Donaldson, based in Merrion Square in Dublin, the people processing our European Trademark application.

'We regret to inform you that your application to register your trademark Piggley Pooh has been opposed by Disney,' said their cover letter to Francis.

We had a separate trademark agent because, while Francis had processed the Irish trademark area, he's always wary of getting into specialised legal areas. He had become an expert in franchising law, thanks to the Piggley Pooh personalised books but trademarking was too important.

Branding is where it's all at, if you're planning to sell not just a character but the merchandise that emerges from a cartoon series about the character. Branding means you can control who uses the name. If, for example, Marks & Spencer want to sell a child's birthday cake with icing on it to look like Nemo out of the movie *Finding Nemo*, not only do M&S have to pay royalties for the use of the image, but they have to satisfy the owners of the brand that their cake is decorated in precisely the colour of the clownfish in the film.

Trademark law is key to intellectual property rights and so, fairly early on, Francis had decided to pull in experts to establish the trademark around the world. As a result, it was McLachlan & Donaldson who took the brunt of the first salvo from Disney. The letter had arrived earlier, but they didn't want to ruin our Christmas, so they hung on to it until January.

Francis was just back at work, all optimistic and positive about the beginning of a new year, when the courier dropped the package at his office in Clane, County Kildare. On this particular day, some premonition made him decide that what was in the envelope was another rejection, and he was bracing himself for that when he realised this communication was infinitely worse. The Disney corporation were objecting to our entire project.

He looked back at the cheery, child-friendly logo at the top of the page and read the letter again, hoping that he might be misunderstanding it. Or even that it was someone's idea of a joke. It was borne in on him however, through the re-reading, that this was no joke. This was a threat from one of the biggest corporations in the world to two of the tiniest minnows in the animated movie stream.

'My God, this is the end,' Francis remembers thinking. 'It

has to be, we can't conceivably even respond to this letter – it's over.'

If it had been me who'd got the letter, I'd have been on to the trademark agents straightaway. Francis waited for two days. That's because, although Francis is very eager and active and good at taking the initiative, he also buys into anger-management and all those pseudo-psychological methods of not jumping too quickly into a situation. What drives me nuts is that whenever he postpones things, the postponement seems to work.

In this case, postponing lifting the phone to Peter McLachlan allowed him to get over what, emotionally, was a shocking blow but – more positively – allowed him to begin to see the letter as an opportunity as well.

'Look, the Disney corporation is interested in you,' he told me. 'They know we're alive, they've heard of our name and the name of our character. My God, this is tremendous.'

'Francis?'

'Yes.'

'They're suing us.'

'That's true, but –'

'Francis, they're *suing* us. The biggest corporation in the entertainment business is suing you and me and Piggley Pooh.'

'Well, technically, they're only suing you and me.'

'So how is that good news?'

'We've arrived!'

'Where?'

'We're on their radar! I mean, Michael Eisner knows who we are. Did you ever think you'd see the day when Michael Eisner would know about Denise and Francis Fitzpatrick from Skryne?'

Reading the letter again, it seemed to me that my life had been a lot happier before Michael Eisner had got to know about me. But, now that he'd got over the initial shock, Francis was on a roll.

'Michael Eisner now knows who we are and that we represent a threat to him, with our character Piggley Pooh,' Francis explained, looking delighted.

I thought this was roughly as positive as having Osama Bin Laden know about us and regard us as a threat. And said so. Francis, striding up and down the sitting-room, wasn't having any of that negative stuff.

'As soon as I realised the real importance of this letter,' he told me, smacking the correspondence off the palm of his hand, 'I started thinking: "How can I utilise this to the benefit of my wife and family?" So I phoned Peter McLachlan. He said he was really sorry and that these are the hazards of international business and what do you want to do about it?'

That was always going to be a no-brainer. Francis was going to fight, and so was I. As I listened to my husband outlining how he was going to meet Peter McLachlan's father, who's a major force in the Irish trademark business, I tried to stamp down the terror evoked in me by the prospect of taking on such a huge business organisation. The prospect, I realised, wasn't just terrifying. It was confusing, too.

Here I was, a mother of toddlers whose instinctive reaction to any of the Disney characters was one of gurgling delight. The Disney name and logo carry warm connotations all over the world, but particularly to parents with small children. Learning to regard Disney as an opponent was going to take some time. I began to take a new interest in what, up to then, had been no more than a name to me.

The Disney family traces its roots back to 1066, when William the Conqueror's invading army took over England. Mercenaries in that army included a few members of the d'Isigny family. Settling down in England, they changed their name to Disney and got on with making money and moving up the social scale. However, when some of them aligned themselves with enemies of King James II, the word went out that their lands were forfeit and they were to be locked up in the Tower of London. Given the times that were in it, there was a good chance their heads might eventually be forfeit, too, so they high-tailed it to Ireland, turned Catholic and lived in Kilkenny. By the nineteenth century, however, they were on the move again, this time across the Atlantic. The Catholicism didn't stick, either. In 1901, Flora Disney gave birth to her fourth son, naming him Walter after the minister in the church where she played the organ.

At around five years of age, Walter began to draw pictures of the animals on the farm where they lived. Because paper was scarce, he used toilet paper. But because toilet paper was scarce, his drawings often disappeared as the paper was put to its originally intended use.

Walt had a particular affection for Porker, one of the pigs in the farmyard. Although in the normal run of things, Porker would never tolerate him riding on her back, when he reappeared having been bed-ridden for a while with chickenpox, it looked as if this might change.

'Porker practically invited me to climb on her back and stayed as peaceful as pie while I crawled aboard – no tantrums, no protests,' he once said. 'She was as proper as a show horse as she cantered me across the farmyard. I was convinced I had tamed her, and she was really glad to see me back. But I should have known better and guessed she was only biding her time … she waded me into the pond, stood quite still for a few seconds, and suddenly tossed me like a tadpole into the deepest and slimiest part of the pond. Then she splashed back to her sty, snorting and snickering in triumph.'

Although Walt the child was fascinated by a pig with a bad attitude named Porker, and although his fame and fortune were founded on a mouse, he actually started off in the animation business with a rabbit named Oswald. And if you think that name could be difficult for audiences, try pronouncing the name of Disney's collaborator: Ub Iwerks. The two of them had to abandon Oswald in a copyright dispute and move on to consider other members of the animal kingdom. Like mice.

Disney didn't actually draw Mickey Mouse. He didn't actually come up with the stories in which the mouse figured. He didn't invent animation. But he had a genius for spotting what would work in the children's market, for refining it, for pulling together people who could provide the skills he lacked, and – in his later years – fronting for his organisation and its films as a benign warm TV presenter. When he died, in 1966, the *New York Times* headline was:

Walt Disney, 65, dies on Coast:
Founded an Empire on a Mouse.

Today, the Walt Disney company is the world's largest leisure corporation. It delivers $25 billion a year to its shareholders, employs more than 100,000 people, worldwide, and has themeparks in Europe, Asia and America drawing millions of visitors annually. Disney World in Florida is America's biggest tourist attraction, and its Parisian equivalent is the most visited European parallel. Shopping malls incorporate Disney outlets, where clothing, DVDs and other souvenirs plastered with characters from the corporation's animated output can be purchased.

Disney himself may be almost fifty years dead, but his enterprise grows exponentially, moving into new markets as they present themselves, so that Disney material is now available on mobile phones and purchasers of those phones can pay for them using a Disney credit card. The corporation owns one of the big three American TV networks, together with cable channel ESPN and its own Disney Channel.

According to film critic Richard Schickel, one factor was key to this entertainment/leisure phenomenon: 'That was Walt Disney's lifelong rage to order, control and keep clean any environment he inhabited. His studio, the last major such facility to be built in Hollywood during its golden age of profitability, was a model of efficient industrial organisation.'

Although words like 'magical', 'heartwarming', 'inspiring' and 'fairytale' tend to be used about his creations, one of Disney's own responses to a reporter, seemed to justify Schickel's judgement. Asked about his most rewarding experience, Disney said it was 'the fact that I was able to build an organisation and *hold it* ...' (Schickel's italics).

One of the biggest contributors to the ongoing success of that organisation is a fat little bear to whom he purchased the rights the year before he died. Winnie the Pooh was one of the inventions of an English writer named A. A. Milne. Winnie the Pooh lives in the Hundred Acre Wood in Sussex, along with his pals, Tigger and Piglet.

When Disney bought all the rights to Milne's bear, they went to work on branding him. Once branded, his identity and reputation could be defended, not just against potential thieves, but against any representation that did the pudgy little bear less than justice. Like Mickey Mouse, Winnie never changes. The colour of his little tee-shirt is always the same, as is the size of the honeypot he gets his head stuck in. He toddles across books, posters and chocolate bars, sits on bedroom ornaments and prances on children's clothes. He's difficult to miss – these days.

But he wasn't difficult to miss when Francis and I were growing up. I never heard of him. In all of the books kicking around our house when I was a child, he never figured. Although some English writers for children, most notably Enid Blyton, were of enormous popularity in the Ireland of the 1960s and 1970s, so that everybody went through phases of *The Famous Five*, A. A. Milne's work did not mesh quite so easily with pre-teens growing up in Ireland at that time.

Yet in January 1999, Disney were opposing our application to register Piggley Pooh as a trademark, filing their first objection in the European Trademark Office in Alicante, Spain.

'They can't be serious,' I said. 'They just can't.'

I hoped it might be some kind of corporate reflex. If some computer somewhere was programmed to react to the word Pooh and generate threatening responses, it was understandable. Once they realised we were just a couple in Ireland taking a character I'd dreamed up as a child and making animated short films about it, they would understand that we represented no threat. Francis shook his head. He was determined to look on the bright side of the challenge, but he wasn't going to let me fool myself: 'Disney are to the entertainment business what Shell are to the oil business or Coca-Cola are to the soft drinks business. Children's entertainment. Animation. Both are Disney's preserve. This is the lion's den.'

'What are we doing in here?' I asked. 'Can we not just get away from this, this dragon, that's going to consume us?'

He stood there, two points of colour high on his cheekbones (always a giveaway that he is tense), looking at the letter as if the intensity of his stare could squeeze some more meaning out of it, or generate a solution to its complaint.

'But we're up and running, aren't we? Don't we have Piggley Pooh registered as a trademark already?'

'They're too late to object in the US,' Francis said slowly. 'We applied for registration there in April 1996. They've objected in Japan, because we applied there. And we would have applied a bit later in –'

I was trying to concentrate, but he could see my eyes glazing over as he went into detail.

He laughed and put the letter away.

'If Disney want a fight, Disney are going to get a fight. Right, Denise?'

'Right, Francis,' I said, with a lot more confidence than I felt.

Within days, Francis was briefing Norman and Peter Mc Lachlan, father and son, and the three of them were beginning to structure the fightback of our little company against the might of Disney. He arrived home on a high.

'The meeting was in 47 Merrion Square,' he told me. 'Georgian building. Big hallway. You walk in and you go into the room on the right and there's a reception desk. Peter came down to me and brought me up to meet his father. When we arrive at his father's office, Norman is standing in front of his huge partner's desk. Everything is in place. It just gives the ordered impression that everything is fine.'

Norman, as I later discovered for myself, is a bespectacled gentleman who looks much younger than his sixty years. Francis was particularly struck by the man's handshake which, he felt, transmitted confidence, power and a sense of 'I'm on your side. This isn't a problem'. Even though Francis was determined to look on the bright side of the challenge, it helped to encounter a trademark advisor who seemed so upbeat.

'It was like getting a really experienced surgeon,' he told me the night of the meeting. 'That's what you want going into a massive heart bypass or a brain tumour surgery. You want someone who has been there before.'

If I *was* going to court against the Disney corporation, I thought, of course I would want the legal equivalent of a major heart surgeon to work on the case. It's just that I really don't want to have a case in the first place. Francis, oblivious to my doubts, was describing the setting for his meeting.

'There's this big boardroom table,' he told me, sketching

it out in gestures. 'I sat down at the head of the table and Norman sat on my right and then Peter sat the other side of me. Bit of banter at the beginning. Things like: "you would have to pick the biggest company in the world!" It breaks the ice and he asks me about Piggley Pooh and how the name was thought of, what we have been doing with the name, have we been using it in business. I'm in no doubt after this meeting that we've got the right guy. I'm really confident now. Norman's attitude is that this is the biggest opponent in the world but we've got a definite case here.'

'How good a case?'

'Pretty strong one. They have done the research as to what reasons Disney could have for opposing us and they're piddling ones. Disney are claiming ownership of Winnie the Pooh, who everyone knows they own and we're not disputing. But they're trying to move ownership of Winnie the Pooh into ownership of Piggley Pooh and that's where their problem lies. Because they're now going to have to start producing evidence as to why they owned Piggley Pooh. Their main argument is that the goodwill in the name Winnie the Pooh is being stolen by us using the word Pooh, so if we had called the character Piggley Winks or Piggley Fitzpatrick or Piggley George, we wouldn't have an objection from them.'

The funny thing, looking back, is that it never occurred to either Francis or me, at that point, to change the name of our pig. It was the easy, obvious thing to do, yet it never surfaced as a possibility. It never struck me as a way to go because I'd been living with this pig and its surname, Pooh, for more than twenty years, so changing it to something else would have been like suddenly calling myself Brittney or Sharon: neither name would have fit. I was used to me as Denise. I was used to Piggley as Pooh.

Francis hadn't quite the relationship with the character that I had. He didn't know Piggley from the time he was a piglet, but changing the name was never a possibility for him either, because of the reaction he had got whenever he used the alliterative moniker; everybody he had spoken to said: 'Piggley Pooh? What a fantastic name! That's a winner.'

As far as we were concerned, we had, in Piggley Pooh, an absolutely winning, blindingly fantastic name and we weren't going to give it up without a struggle. We certainly weren't going to go for any of the options that would have deflected Disney's hostility.

To have done so would have made me feel filthy – as if I had tried to steal something that had never been mine and been caught out.

Once he was clear that we weren't prepared to take the easy, obvious escape hatch of re-naming the pig, Norman McLachlan concentrated on our prospects should this come to court.

'If you discount the fact that it's Disney,' he told Francis. 'If you imagine that it was just Joe Bloggs versus Denise and Francis Fitzpatrick, this is a 50/50 and probably 60/40 in your favour. But even against Disney, you could win this case.'

Buoyed up by that advice, Francis had a growing sense of excitement, not just about the prospects of beating them in open court, but of the massive media blitz opportunity it represented. No one had heard of Denise Fitzpatrick but everyone had heard of Disney and for them to take an interest in us, even if the interest was negative, was going to make us – and our little pig – famous. If we set out to pay for the publicity that would come out of this, Francis calculated, it would cost us between five and ten million dollars.

'That reminds me,' I said, clearing the table of our teacups. 'Did he ask you about money?'

Francis shook his head: 'I brought up the issue of money.'

I looked at him, mystified as to why he would have raised payment when he knew we were so short of money. If the trademark expert hadn't mentioned cash, why bring it up?

'It's always a good tactic to bring it up yourself to give the impression that you've made provision for the fees.'

'But you haven't.'

'At this moment, we have no chance of paying him. But that's for another day. All I said was: "Listen, I've been speaking to my bank and you might just give me an indication as to what you require over the next three months so that can be ready for you."'

The three of them at the table ended up working out whether the bills would be issued on a monthly or a quarterly basis, with Francis being very suave in his preference for quarterly as better for his planning process. The reality was that whether they billed monthly, quarterly or annually, their prospects of getting anything in return, in the short term, were not great.

But, listening to Francis' account of the meeting, I hadn't a qualm about that aspect of the situation. Nor had Francis, who had been reading up about Denis O'Brien, who had just become a multi-millionaire, having started, as did Michael O'Leary, as assistant to Tony Ryan of GPA. It was the era for risk-taking; indeed, it was probably the first in Irish business history that favoured risk-takers. Up to the Celtic Tiger era, Ireland wasn't hot on entrepreneurship or business gambling. The ultimate ambition for many people was a permanent and pensionable job in the civil service.

But men like Denis O'Brien were now breaking through to breathtaking success. Not only were they succeeding, they were also talking to journalists about their unsuccessful years and about earlier ventures that had gone belly-up. Francis was fascinated by O'Brien's account of launching his first TV shopping channel in the US. It hadn't worked and he had found himself haemorrhaging at the rate of £12,000 a month which he didn't have. Now, the Fitzpatricks were haemorrhaging at the rate of £16,000 a month.

We were seriously in debt, owing at least £250,000 to several banks.

Paul Dubsky, a Clongowes past pupil and friend, asked Paul McGuinness of U2 for help. McGuinness kindly provided Francis with the name of the law firm representing U2 in America and gave Francis a letter of introduction. The relevant lawyer at the firm responded positively, saying he felt we had a very good case against Disney. He said he was prepared to represent us but that they would require an advance payment of $50,000. Unfortunately this was $50,000 too far for us.

We didn't even have a house at that time. We had the piece of land which we still own that my father had given us when we got married and it was the one shining beacon in the whole dark landscape. It was in a place called Branstown which is three miles from my parents' house. The idea was we would apply for planning permission and build there. But when we applied for permission, we were refused, so we couldn't do anything with the land. The local authority, Meath County Council, was issuing more or less one hundred per cent refusals to planning applications at that time – they just didn't want any what were called 'one-off houses'.

Their thinking was that it was better to build houses, and supply the services required by those houses, on the edge of existing villages or towns. A few years later, the government changed the rules, so that one-off housing became acceptable.

I had added to our original plot another six acres purchased from my father. The main reason we bought it was that I knew he wanted to sell it, but I didn't want it to go to anyone outside our family. This meant, at the time Disney fired their first salvo at us, that we were in an odd situation. We didn't have our own home, but we had seven acres of land. We were paying my father for that land, but owning it would allow us to leverage money if we needed it, because land appreciates all the time. (The traditional advice is to buy land because they're not making any more of it.)

In theory, then, as Francis looked at financing a war with Disney, he could afford to think positively. Guys like Denis O'Brien and Michael O'Leary and a bunch of dot com entrepreneurs were all over the business pages, taking risks and making millions. The two of us owned land. We had a good relationship with our bankers. As a result of his father being a banker, Francis always took the view that, no matter what happened in his life, he needed to have good relations with his bank manager and we always strove to do that. Of course, by that time, it was a case of bank managers – plural. Between Piggley Pooh, parenting, land purchase and the costs of our as yet unbuilt new house, we now had borrowings with Allied Irish Bank, Ulster Bank and Bank of Ireland.

Because Francis was in the legal business, he could also expect, in the normal run of things, that every now and then along would come a major case where he could charge as much as €200,000. The only difficulty was that to earn that kind of fee, you have to do the work. As we mustered our forces to fight off the Disney corporation, this was emerging as a problem. Francis wasn't going to have the time to generate income.

We were cash poor. We were time poor. We were rich in dreams but the biggest purveyor of dreams was threatening to destroy them. We also had high hopes of a production deal with a company called Cascade but what was going to happen to that?

Chapter Eleven

CASCADE AND CATASTROPHE

Signing the option with Cascade in 1998 was one of the high points in the development of Piggley Pooh. By getting a subsidiary of the extremely successful Scottish Media Group on board, we had achieved much more than what our television advisers in Ireland believed was possible: we had a signed contract. True, it was only a signed *option* contract, but it was still an agreement with a major multi-national who had delivered several multi-million-dollar animated series with no great difficulty. As far as the two of us were concerned, we had made it.

When the big shadow of Disney fell across the situation however – Tinkerbell in jackboots – the two of us immediately realised that this had implications for Cascade's plans.

At this point, I was helping my father with accounts, spending all my time on the farm with my parents, with Klaragh and with our second baby, Daniel. For about a month, Francis would come home each evening and we would kick around the moral and business implications of telling Cascade the full story about Disney. If we relied on the odds presented by the trademark expert, Norman Mc Lachlan, we could decide not to tell Cascade anything, since it wasn't going to affect them, given the likelihood that we would win. But what if the odds didn't play out as we hoped? What if we didn't win?

On the one hand, discretion was the better part of valour. On the other hand, neither Francis nor I was comfortable concealing something from a company that was so enthusiastic about the whole concept. Honesty, we decided, wasn't just the better policy, it was the only policy. So off Francis went to tell Cascade that Disney was obsessing about their ownership of a syllable: Pooh.

Of course, by the time Francis got off the plane in Scotland, he had got himself to a point where he was ready to sell, rather than reveal. He arrived into their offices and pitched to them the benefits of being sued by an international corporation.

'Disney want something we own,' he told them, truthfully. 'Maybe there's something in it for you. Piggley Pooh is even more valuable than when you first got enthused about him.'

As it turned out, he didn't have to do a hard sell. The Cascade people weren't unduly concerned about the name, *per se*. They said the name wasn't as important as the overall package represented by the series they were making. That overall package was based on the values and simple insights of farm life in Ireland as seen by the animals and linked to Irish mythology. That was the essence of the story that they were telling. They weren't terribly concerned with the name.

That came as a surprise to Francis. It was a welcome surprise. Our production company were unconcerned at the possibility that Disney might force a name change in the central character.

'Well, look, if we have to change the name, so be it,' Cascade's management told Francis. They were very cool about it. Their attitude took a lot of pressure off both of us. Even though each of us – particularly me – had a preference for the name Pooh, we now knew that we could change the pig's surname if we had to, without it delaying the immediate production plans.

In fact, at this point, changing the pig's name would have been by far the simplest option. But every time we looked at that option, one of us would say to the other: 'Hold on. We have a right to it. Why should we abandon something that someone else coincidentally came up with? Why walk away from magic?'

There was certainly magic in some aspect of our little character, which was the top attraction at the Cannes Television Festival on the Cascade stand that year. It gave me tremendous satisfaction. It was like winning the World Cup to see my creation on the Cascade stand. Cascade had maybe ten other projects but they were nowhere to be seen, because the only thing they were selling was Piggley Pooh. They had a storyboard made up, a beautiful brochure and a series of outline stories.

Great progress was happening on the production side. Very little was happening on the litigation side. Things happened very, *very* slowly. At first, I thought this might indicate that Disney's heart (assuming they had one) wasn't in the effort to crush the Fitzpatricks. Francis quickly disabused me of that notion: 'In terms of Disney, the game is always protracted,' he warned me. 'It's "let the other guy bleed to death, we're up here for seventy-five years, he'll be gone in seven months." So that's the way they're playing the game.'

But, at the same time, we had to keep our banks onside. The best way to do that was to get them to sit down with Cascade's top people so that our banks could get a sense of the scale of what was planned.

In June 1999, we orchestrated a lunch in the Allied Irish Bank Centre, attended by Cascade. We had hired a limousine to pick the executives up at Dublin Airport. No money, but hiring limousines … it was surreal. But we believed we had to do it because it would impress both them and the bank. Which it did. I remember us arriving at the bank and passersby looking sideways to see what celeb was getting out of the limousine. Inside the bank centre, AIB had a sumptuous lunch laid on. Several courses, served by white-gloved waiters.

Cascade's lead guy, a Welshman named Ian Jones, was very impressed. He was also very impressive about the Piggley Pooh project. Elizabeth Partyka was the other executive and the two of them worked hard and impressively on our behalf with AIB. The impact, for the bank, was phenomenal. They were getting a real understanding of how we were actually forming the cartoon series. They were learning all about Cascade's full-time sales people and about their partners in production houses in Australia, Canada and the UK who wanted to share in the making of Piggley Pooh. The Cascade people were on top of their game, sitting there, explaining about German tax-based funds that would come in and deliver twenty per cent of the budget.

Cascade left our bankers in no doubt that they were promoting Piggley Pooh to an extent that no one else was. They were promoting a dream on the back of my dream. At this type of meeting, Francis would always come in with input about the Irish tax concession, Section 481, which was established to attract film production companies. The bankers could see that while there was risk involved, we had joined up with an experienced production company which was part of a major holding company with links all over the world. In addition, they knew that Disney regarded us as sufficiently threatening to want to block our progress, but they also knew our prospects of beating Disney off – and gaining from the resultant publicity – could be regarded as positive.

They could see that while we were a young couple with mad dreams of creativity and money and fame and publicity and pizzazz, we were nonetheless professionals who had taken the advice of the best experts from the beginning and accordingly were realistic in our optimism. Mary Leonard from KPMG Corporate Finance, the number one film business expert in Ireland, had told us at the very beginning of this whole story, back in the mid-1990s, that Francis shouldn't give up his day job, because Piggley Pooh starring on international screens was a ten million to one shot.

At that AIB lunch, Francis quoted Mary Leonard to the banker to make it clear to them that we took the worst case scenario into account at all times and were realistic about what we were doing. In advance, he had sold Cascade's expertise to the bankers to make them comfortable with the risks he wanted them to take.

Ian Jones and Elizabeth Partyka being so impressive had a knock-on benefit for the Fitzpatricks. Referred credibility meant that the bank became even more impressed with us: the couple who had delivered one of the biggest production companies in the world to their offices. We had a signed deal with this company. Now, AIB could feel comfortable when asked to release the Section 481 monies at the appropriate time.

Afterwards, we visited Cascade's premises in Glasgow to discuss scripts with their full team and to flesh out the characters. This was a considerable challenge to me, because I knew all of the characters but, because I was inexperienced as a scriptwriter, I tended to assume that everybody else knew the characters the same way and, of course, they didn't. The Cascade team were good at mining for the details that were obvious to me. They peppered me with questions about what the characters did, what they were like, what their personality was like, what was Piggley Pooh like.

I told them he was a great seanchaí.

'A great *what*?'

I laughed and explained that Irish culture is strong on the role of the storyteller and how long before television, Ireland had a tradition of older men and women telling stories by the fireside.

I had always felt that Piggley Pooh should be a seanchaí. When I saw him in my head, it was as an older pig with glasses, telling the stories of when he was young. I hoped that the stories would incorporate some of the legends I'd been told as a child – the Salmon of Knowledge, for example, and I was delighted when the Cascade people agreed.

They also went along with the idea that where the animals lived should not be a polished, high-tech farm. Instead, I wanted it to be a rundown, very eco-friendly farm where real animals did real work in a way that was friendly to the environment. I had this funny contrast in my mind of a Hitler-type farm up on a hill nearby where the cows were marching round training and they would only be accepted on that farm if they had the best quality milk.

The Cascade people wanted a love story between Pigaleen and Piggley Pooh, which was fine by me.

But I also wanted Piggley Pooh to believe that he had been switched at birth with another piglet and that he had royal blood as a result. This, again, refers back to Irish mythology and the 'changeling', where the fairies were believed to snatch babies from the cradle and replace them with one of their own. Making Piggley a changeling meant that he shouldn't really have been on a rundown old farm: he should have been up on the hill in the Hitler farm, but he wouldn't have treated the animals up there as badly as they were being treated.

The Cascade writers were picking and choosing between various possible story lines and it was all go. We were so busy exploring every detail of Piggley's life and times that we failed to register the importance of something happening in the background of Cascade's operation. A new chairman arrived at the helm of their parent company, Scottish Media Group, and brought in his own team. Ian Jones moved on. None of that seemed terribly important to our ongoing project. Nor did the fact that soon a couple of months had gone by without much further contact with Cascade.

Our next meeting was to allow us to meet the new man on the job for Cascade, Adrian Howells. We went to London to the Cascade offices near Piccadilly, where we were shown into what looked to me like a disused store-room. I may exaggerate a bit, but not much. Welcoming and well-appointed it was not. My antenna were picking up a bad signal long before Adrian arrived.

'I've some very bad news for you,' he told us. 'The company has decided to close down the production arm.'

'Close down Cascade?'

He nodded. The incoming chairman and his team were not interested in a production arm that wasn't contributing serious profits to the bottom line.

'I've got three months in my job,' Adrian told us glumly. 'And then, that's it for me, too.'

We couldn't believe it. We just couldn't believe that a bunch of total strangers had moved into the company that had hung its hat on our character, and decided to close the whole thing down. I was sorry for Adrian, having to deal with this kind of stuff while working out his own notice, but I was angry with him, too. Angry because he should have given us some advance warning that we were not coming to an ordinary script meeting. But my anger went wider than Adrian. I couldn't understand why they couldn't have had a more structured meeting with a lot more people – senior people – involved, instead of having us dismissed by someone who was on the way out the door himself.

'What kind of a way is this to treat production partners?' I demanded, gesturing at the chaotic, scruffy office we were in. 'This is disgraceful. It's totally unprofessional.'

'I'm sorry, but it's really not my fault,' Adrian said. 'I'm only in the job a few weeks, and couldn't have anticipated –'

'Maybe not, but Ian Jones must have known,' I retorted. 'It's perfectly clear *now* why he departed when he did and said so little to us. He was moving on to Granada and he didn't even warn us. He was our partner and he effectively got into the lifeboat without us.' In fairness to Ian Jones he had a young family himself and was desperately trying to survive. But at this point I was taking no prisoners.

We were facing total collapse of our partnership, absolute abandonment by one side of the entire project. Out of the blue. No warning. We were in a position like the developer of a shopping mall faced with the pull-out of an anchor tenant like Tesco, Dunnes Stores or KMart. If you don't have that kind of magnet, you don't have the shopping centre. Our anchor tenant had now been closed down.

But even as I raged at Adrian, Francis was already looking for a lifeline. Cascade had produced scripts, storyboards and other materials showing Piggley Pooh in an advanced stage of development. Adrian had brought this armful of paperwork to the meeting, perhaps as a form of comfort – something to hold on to – because it self-evidently wasn't going to be discussed. Francis desperately wanted to take that material with him when we left the grotty office we were in and flew home to Ireland.

So when I ground to a halt, he started to talk. His tone was quite different to mine. The voice was calm, the attitude agreeable. I couldn't figure what he was doing, but I know Francis well enough to guess that, although he was undoubtedly as furious as I was, he had an objective in view and I shouldn't get in his way. I sat silently while he expressed great personal sympathy for Adrian.

Very tough, he observed, for Adrian to have arrived into this situation. Unfortunate, to be promoted to Ian's job and then have the whole thing folded up around him. Particularly unfortunate when Adrian had not been responsible for

Cascade's lack of positive contribution to its parent company's bottom line.

Adrian began to relax somewhat. He nodded dumbly as Francis speculated that he must be feeling pretty awful. One of the things we might do for him, Francis suggested, was talk to RTÉ on his behalf. Suss out possibilities for a job for him. Adrian was now all warmed up and grateful. I was all warmed up and hateful. I'd have cheerfully strangled Adrian and then gone looking for Ian Jones to do the same to him. But I sat in boiling silence while Francis worked the two of them to a position where it was inevitable that Adrian would slide the bundle of paperwork across the cluttered desk to Francis and we would all head to the door.

I made a point of dusting off my skirt, in order to send a message to Adrian that it was bad enough to renege on a deal, but to make the announcement in what was little more than a storeroom was gratuitously offensive. I might as well not have bothered. He was so relieved to see the back of us and so grateful to Francis for being civil about it, that anything as subtle as a skirt dust-off wasn't going to register with him.

The two of us flagged a cab and got ourselves back to the airport, Francis filling me in, on the way, about what he had salvaged and how we could use it in the future. I sat on the plane, my eyes full of tears, nodding and not hearing a word he said. The way I saw it, we were coming away from what should have been a meeting devoted to onward progress, to getting my little pig up on the big screen, and instead, like Alice in *Through the Looking Glass*, the path had shaken itself like a snake and put us facing in a quite different direction.

We were now in serious trouble. It wasn't that we were back at square one. We were way *behind* square one. Sisyphus – the figure from Greek mythology who kept rolling this large stone up the hill only to see it rolling down time and again – was seemingly our partner on this project. Francis had listened to Mary Leonard and had kept doing his day job but, inevitably, he hadn't been able to build it up. Its growth had been on hold while we promoted Piggley Pooh. After we came back home to Meath, Francis found himself heading off to his law practice in Kildare at six each morning, laden with misery over Cascade and Disney. Even the location for that law practice had turned out to be less than productive. When we'd picked the location, it seemed like a good idea to have one office in Dublin, which was twenty-two miles away, and another in a satellite town (Kildare), which was twenty-two miles away from both Meath and Dublin, so we'd be operating in a triangle. Also, the thoroughbred horse world is based in Kildare and we assumed the Kildare office would allow the practice to become big in horse racing, which is a business with a lot of wealthy people in it. It never worked out. Francis never got one horse racing client.

'How do I get through today?' he would think, driving to his Kildare office. 'Well, today won't actually be that bad. No one's going to come looking for money because I'd have got notices from creditors and the revenue and the sheriff – they'll all give advance warning. So today will be OK from that point of view.'

Ironically, each day was OK, too, in terms of surroundings. His Kildare office mightn't be attracting the rich race-horsing clientele we'd both hoped it would, but it was much larger and more luxurious than he could afford in Dublin. So, in beautiful surroundings, Francis concentrated on cash-flow. That meant conveyancing. To this day, if you say that word to him – conveyancing – he shrivels.

'Conveyancing is mind-numbing stuff,' he maintains. 'Dealing with titles to buildings and land. Horrible.'

He did it and he did it professionally. But each day, as he closed the office door behind him, he would make one small promise to himself.

'When Piggley Pooh is up and running, I will never, ever, touch conveyancing again as long as I live.'

As well as raising our family and working with my father, I was trying to cope with emerging complications in our personalised book business. Although the Stephen's Green outlet was still doing splendidly, some of the franchises around the country had proven to be more trouble than they were worth, and so they had been closed. This meant that even combining the income from our remaining outlet with Francis' income from practising law, could not begin to make an impact on our steadily growing losses.

Now that Cascade had gone under, we were back to the beginning, in terms of persuading production houses to be interested in Piggley Pooh. This, inevitably, caused us to spend a fortune on contacting people, on travel and on presentations. The costs mounted inexorably.

We were so badly in debt that Francis had begun to do the unthinkable – ask relatives and friends to lend him money, beginning with his father. Seeing Francis two or three times a week as they always do, his parents had to know their son was under financial stress.

'How are things going?' his father would ask him. 'You making any money out of your law practice? Is everything ok?'

Eventually, Francis admitted everything was not OK.

'No, Dad, I could do with some cash,' he admitted. 'Just a bit of a cashflow problem.'

'How much are you talking about?'

'Could you give me a few thousand?'

'How much is "a few"?' (Remember, Francis' dad was a bank manager, trained to be precise and accurate ...)

'Can you give me ten?'

'Well, that's going to be difficult.' Long silence. 'But, yes, I'm good for that.'

He wrote a cheque for £10,000 and gave it to Francis, who popped it into the office account. That would keep us going for a couple of months on the basis that we would only pay bills when the final-final demand notices came. We were on survival rations, no new clothes, pay electricity, phone, gas only when they came to cut us off. This was a war and my young children and myself were in the front line. When conveyancing fees came in, Francis paid his father back. But then, a few months later, the pattern would repeat, with his father sometimes lending us £20,000 and getting it back and then lending another ten or twenty. Or in one case, £30,000.

Then Francis went to other friends, particularly good friends such as Brendan Heneghan, a partner in William Fry Solicitors. Brendan was a very good friend to Francis and to this day would bankroll him if he needed it. Brendan would lend money to Francis and – in common with Francis' father – would get paid back, then borrowed from again. It was a mad dance of one step forward, two steps back.

No matter how generous or trusting friends and family are when they lend you money, it doesn't stop you feeling like hell about borrowing from them. The two of us felt like hell most of the time. We were in the dumps and felt worthless – it is humiliating to go cap in hand to a friend and obviously we wouldn't have done it if there was any other way but there wasn't. It didn't help that we had involved good people like the McConnells, who had shown such faith in us and our character, and who – like us – now stood to lose a great deal of money.

We were petrified of the consequences for us. The consequences of losing a lot of money would begin with bankruptcy and proceed to the loss of Francis' legal career, because in Ireland if a lawyer is declared bankrupt, he/she is struck off the roll of solicitors and cannot practise. But for some reason, crazy as it may seem, neither of these dire possibilities was our major point of fear. What we dreaded most was the thought of not being able to repay friends and family. Our loss would be our just desserts for believing absolutely in our project, but our friends and family would have been innocent victims of our addiction to Piggley Pooh.

Life suddenly turned into an endless series of meetings with banks. AIB. Bank of Ireland. Ulster Bank. Francis himself was like a character in an animated cartoon skating on ice so thin that big cracks keep opening up on all sides of him. He had to keep going faster and faster, smiling wider and wider. He had to convey great confidence in the cinematic future of Piggley Pooh, a wannabe character who, in four years, hadn't made any progress beyond starring in a three-minute promotional film and appearing in McConnells' lovely brochure.

No bank manager is ever going to be comfortable banking an imaginary pig. Our bank managers were getting acutely uncomfortable about it. Francis had to keep begging for time and getting it. Grudgingly.

The big problem was what to do with the time he got out of the banks. It was like having your entry to the marathon accepted and then realising someone has cemented you to the floor. In theory, you may have the freedom to win, but in practical terms, you're not moving.

By their actions, which were now well-publicised throughout the film-making community, Disney had cemented the Fitzpatrick feet to the floor, and Piggley Pooh's four feet, likewise. There seemed to be a real prospect that the whole lot of us would end up like Henrietta Hen, living in a wheelbarrow.

I had read somewhere about the late British prime minister, Harold MacMillan, that he had shrugged off setbacks throughout his career by pointing out that 'it is the grit in the oyster which forms the pearl'.

We had plenty of grit in our life. But the chances of it forming a pearl seemed to be diminishing by the day. And all the determined optimism in the world didn't seem to improve those chances.

Chapter Twelve

HARD TIMES

From the time we had entered the Cartoon Forum in Connemara in September 1996 we were fully committed entrepreneurs. The two of us were born to be entrepreneurs and we'd done well with our personalised book venture. But any good entrepreneur takes a joy in risk and, I found, as a mother with two young children and a third on the way, the joy in risk was diminishing for me. The 'devil may care' attitude of the entrepreneur does not sit well with motherhood. Motherhood is all about protecting and nurturing your children in a safe and loving environment.

We were engaged in a battle for survival with the largest leisure corporation in the world, hell bent on destroying us. This was not a forum for my children and whilst the two of us did everything we could to shield them from the financial difficulties we were in, sometimes I felt hopeless and despaired of ever being able to look at a bank statement that didn't scream with red ink: *Pay now or we'll foreclose. Pay now or we'll pull your facilities. Pay now or we'll sluice you down the tubes.*

Since December 1996, things had becoming increasingly difficult. In simple terms, we had run out of money. We were surviving on credit. We were always looking to our next loan from a bank, from a friend, from a credit union, from anyone or anything that would give us money to go on. We were like addicts, addicted to our beautiful project to an extent that robbed us of pride. We knew all the arguments. We knew what reason and sense demanded that we should do, yet nothing persuaded either of us to call time on a project that had – in the words of our first accountant, Mary Leonard, of KPMG Corporate Finance – about a ten million to one shot of success.

On a daily basis Francis was on the front line. He was the magician, the rain man, and the miracle worker. He had to produce money out of thin air as this is the only way that an under-funded, under-resourced project can keep going. The fact that he did it is one of the reasons his all-time favourite movie is the John Grisham thriller, *Rain Man*, in which Danny de Vito and Matt Damon star as attorneys on the make who join a law firm which is a front for an ambulance-chasing lower-end group of attorneys who 'must make rain' in order to survive. Matt Damon is given the job of sitting in a hospital for the summer trying to attract injured patients to engage the law firm. It's a funny film for lawyers. It's a funny film for people who have survived living hand-to-mouth. I'm not sure either of us would have found it funny around Christmas 1997, one of the most difficult times in our life together.

Although the Piggley Pooh shop had its best trading times at Christmas, as all retail stores do, the revenues from Piggley Pooh were simply too tiny to make any impact on the acres of debt built up around us. Allied Irish Banks, where Francis has his law practice account, had advised him in no uncertain terms that he needed to substantially reduce his overdraft. The way he had been operating it would be tolerated no longer.

It was time for him to start behaving himself. That was the message from AIB. It was also the message from Bank of Ireland. Ulster Bank were not that happy about how over-drawn we were with *them* either.

I used to have a nightmare around this time, of lying in a bed in a hospital in Dublin, perhaps St Vincent's Hospital.

In the dream, I was in a coma with four tubes sticking out of me. Except that, instead of intravenous fluid and/or blood or proteins being pumped into me, the opposite was happening: my blood was being siphoned out to four different containers, each carefully labelled with the logos of Allied Irish Bank, Bank of Ireland, Ulster Bank and the Meath Credit Union. As soon as I went to sleep, in went the four tubes. The only problem was that when I would wake up, I would feel as exhausted as if I had given several pints of blood to each of them, yet was facing a day in which no inroads had been made on our mountain of indebtedness.

We had become particularly dependent on Bank of Ireland, Navan, where my family had banked for a number of generations. The district manager of the bank, Pat Hamill, was based in Navan. Unlike a normal branch manager he had the ability to give an on the spot decision for a loan in excess of €30,000, as he was in charge of a number of branches. Pat was someone I had known as our bank manager for a number of years. When we first approached him to fund our Piggley Pooh shop in 1995 he was delighted to facilitate us. Now, as the darkest hours of our financial survival approached, he could see from the statements that we were in difficulty. Francis warned me on St Stephen's Day, 26 December 1997, that I should be aware that we had written cheques to cover necessary expenses which could not be met. He had written these cheques to the ESB, the gas company and other essential suppliers because they had to be paid. In addition, some business suppliers also received our humble uncertified cheques. By using the strategy of postdating them to 1 January 1998 we had a further seven to ten days to find the money to cover the cheques as Irish banks close for a number of days over the Christmas period.

Armageddon, in terms of our banking relationship, arrived on 4 January 1998. The banks had re-opened and

Francis spent the entire day of the fourth out there looking for survival money. He spoke to friends and family, the credit unions, AIB Bank, Ulster Bank, and Bank of Ireland at Navan. All had been unable to help. We had no plan B – we now had to face the music and accept that our credibility as business people was over. Once cheques bounce, your reputation with suppliers and the banks descends to nothing – no one is going to provide credit, cash is the name of the game, cash which we couldn't get.

It looked as if we might have to ask to move in with my parents or siblings. I could imagine them welcoming us, but I couldn't imagine ever holding my head up again afterwards: after four years of marriage and two children, to have to beg for readmission to the family home ...

Francis was just as appalled by this prospect as I was. But he nonetheless kidded me about it: 'Didn't you always want to move home to Skryne to your parents?' he would ask. 'Well, now Disney have made that dream come true.'

He was lucky I didn't brain him.

The morning of 5 January arrived. Francis phoned Pat Hamill at Bank of Ireland Navan at 10 a.m. He was operating on the military theory that attack is the best method of defence and on the belief that you don't look like a loser if you make the first move.

The butterflies were working overtime as I stood by Francis' side by the phone in our house. I heard Pat's firm voice as he reiterated what he had already told Francis yesterday that the bank could not offer the further facility of €50,000 we had requested. Stone cold silence from our end. Nothing to do but watch as the car crash happened. We were trapped in the headlights. I mentally started arranging boxes for our clothes, furniture, belongings. I had a massive phonecall to make after this and I started to rehearse it in my mind:

'Mum? It's Denise here – can I come home to live with

you and Dad with Klaragh and Daniel? For how long? I don't know. Maybe forever. Francis is going to stay in Dublin with his parents. My family is going to be parted by debt.'

Even though I was only mentally rehearsing what I would say to my mother, the humiliation of it made me cry. I could not believe that I was witnessing the breakup of my beloved family, I was horrified at the damage it would do our children.

Through my tears, I saw Francis nodding frantically to whatever was being said to him on the phone.

'Pat, thanks a million,' he was saying. 'We really appreciate this and we won't let you down.'

I couldn't believe it. The marines had arrived. We were safe for another while. This wonderful bank manager earned a place in our affections forever. He had advised that Bank of Ireland were unable to offer us the €50,000 but, having reviewed our position overnight, had decided to provide €30,000 to us over six months. I made a promise to myself there and then despite the euphoria of financial survival that I would never ever let my family or children be threatened by this again. We have remained loyal to the Bank of Ireland since that moment and still bank with Pat's successor, Vivienne Rountree, who took up the cudgels on our behalf and continues to back our ventures.

From 5 January 1998 onwards I became a budget shopper. I went to the cheapest shops, I questioned the need for any purchase, I compared prices. It was hand-me-down time. We might be engaged in a million-dollar project, but in truth we were worse than penniless. At the same time, we couldn't afford to be seen as penniless, so we ended up effectively living parallel lives. We had no income, were surviving on borrowings and yet Francis had to live the life of the high-spending, Armani-suited TV executive at Cannes and Las Vegas and then live the rest of the time at budget level in Ireland.

Our closest friends and family were concerned. They

could see the fallacy of our existence. We were taking pot shots at the largest leisure corporation in the world, trying to nurture an embryonic television series which even wealthy business people wouldn't touch due to the high failure rate, *and* trying to live a normal suburban life. Francis' parents couldn't understand why a lawyer would risk everything to go to the casino of the television industry and put all his chips on black 38 which was likely to lose anyway. All of the people who cared for us found occasions to gently suggest to Francis or to me that there were other ways of living which would not lead to an early grave.

Their kindness overwhelmed us, particularly as many of them were people from whom we had borrowed. I was mortified as Francis kept borrowing money from pals, from family, from anyone he could get his hands on. It was like being married to a gambling addict or someone hooked on heroin. Except that I was in the addiction with him. Of course I could, and did, make noises about stopping the borrowing, but they were half-hearted noises which were promptly met by Francis with health warnings about dignity.

'This project cannot succeed if we have any dignity left,' he would tell me. 'Dignity is the death of most projects.'

I remembered a time when I didn't even have to think about dignity. It was an entitlement. But when you're borrowing from your father, your mother, your best pals and are even willing to beg money from acquaintances, dignity is no longer your entitlement. I was dying inside, all the time, wondering about the reactions of people who had lent us money. Maybe they would want us to be going around in second-hand clothes and if they saw Francis all dolled up for one of his big meetings, might think we were in denial and really didn't understand how bad our situation was.

All the old cliché jokes suddenly took on a new reality. It is true that banks will only lend you money when you don't need it; that they will only give you an umbrella when the sun is shining. We needed to convince them on every occasion that the sun was shining. It was like a new career in the theatre. I became a better actor than René Zellweger, and Francis could have competed with John Travolta when it came to convincing performances and giving them a little fancy footwork while he was at it.

The two of us would deliver Oscar-worthy performances in each bank manager's office. Each performance would have been rehearsed in great detail beforehand. Like good actors, we learned to improvise: What would we do if he said X? Like good TV stations, we constantly researched our audience, so that we gave them what we knew would meet their needs. We would suggest, or rather insist, that we meet our bank manager prior to him summoning us in to complain about the overdraft being severely breached. We worked hard to convey our concern that the bank would not lose out and that we were committed to complying with the facilities in a very mature and rounded fashion – at some stage in the not-too-distant future. We might not have had a lot in common with St Augustine, but we were just like him when it came to postponement of virtue. Augustine asked God to make him chaste – 'but not yet'.

We actively sought to meet with our banks every quarter or at least every six months. Coming up to the appointment, the two of us got into character. I would dress to the nines and adopt my Smurfit-like air of efficiency and authority. Francis would ensure that his one pinstripe suit was properly dry-cleaned and ready. I would have my hair done and my nails polished.

Wardrobe taken care of, we would move on to props. When we marched into the bank, it was vital that we have all the necessary asset/cashflow/revenue forecasts with us, delivering a perception of absolute efficiency. In addition we would bring with us all the recent newspaper articles which carried any mention of our own project. Our image, reflected back from media, was strong and credible; *Never mind the reality, taste the coverage.* We would also make sure to bring with us any relevant coverage of the Disney corporation, having trained ourselves as hawk-eyed observers of international mass media and business media.

One of Francis' favourite articles about Disney was a feature in *Forbes Magazine* in 1999 in which the Disney balance sheet was examined and in particular the *Winnie the Pooh* earnings revealed. The article clearly stated that Disney made revenues of $6bn per annum, year on year, from *Winnie the Pooh*. Smacking that cutting down in front of our financiers, we would of course make the point that since we were in a battle with Disney it must be for ownership of this $6bn per annum. To be honest, neither of us had copped on to this particular article. (One of Francis' good friends, Cormac Lucy, had come across it and had kindly forwarded it to Francis. For his reward, Cormac received our usual standard Piggley Pooh pack which included a Polo shirt carrying the logo of our character. On the night before Cormac's wedding to Ciara in 2002 he proudly wore his Piggley Pooh t-shirt which made us all feel great. Irrationally great. But great, nonetheless.)

There was a distinct and gigantic gulf between the *Forbes* article on Disney's $6bn a year earnings and our lack of ability to pay even the most essential elementary bills such as gas, light, heat, telephone until the very last minute. We put off payment, on some occasions, until we were literally cut off. Our friends and colleagues sometimes couldn't reach us on our landline, not because there was a problem with the phone or the phoneline but because we had been unable to pay the bill. We began to look longingly at the queues leading up to ATMs in the street, remembering with sweet nostalgia when it had been safe to stick a card in one of them and request cash. Now, like knowledgeable crooks, we were hyper-conscious of only two possibilities associated with the 'hole in the wall' machines. The first was that they would swallow the card and never give it back. The second was that the hidden camera would take footage of us and that we'd see it on the TV *Crimeline* programme.

We were on a never-ending cycle of spending way beyond our means to keep in the game of presenting Piggley Pooh at the Cannes Television Festival and at Las Vegas. These are two of the most expensive cities in the world and particularly so during a television conference weekend. In Cannes, for example, Francis would stay in the two-star Royale Azurene Hotel. The hotel, which is well located but extremely two-star, would cost approximately €600 for the conference. After that inevitable expenditure, Francis had to make every other saving possible. I didn't go to the festival. That saved money, and in any event I couldn't go because I had to mind our children. Francis would save the bread roll and tiny pat of butter that came with the airline meal or eat in McDonalds. Everybody else in the television industry could splash out thousands on the famous Cannes restaurants. Francis ate like a pauper.

While Francis didn't mind eating like a pauper, he could not afford not to take his potential clients out to those same fabulous restaurants and a weird pattern emerged. One day, he would have a slap-up meal with people he was trying to interest in Piggley Pooh, desperately trying to swallow much-needed protein while concentrating on doing his hard-sell. The next day, his nutrition would come from a stale airline bun. We were playing a desperately dangerous game, but there was no other game in town and we had to keep at it. We were hamsters on a wheel of borrowing, a cycle of debt that we couldn't get off.

Financial pressures were eating away at our souls. But what was most difficult was the amount of time we were forced to spend apart. I really felt for Francis when he had to get up at unearthly hours in the morning such as 4 a.m. to catch a flight at Dublin Airport to go to Luton to connect with the Easyjet flight to Cannes for the festival. Francis was unable to afford the direct Aer Lingus flight which most of the senior television executives from Ireland took from Dublin to Nice. Instead, by booking a month in advance on Ryanair and connecting on Easyjet, he could get to Cannes for about €50.

We were fortunate that our worst financial days happened to coincide with the explosion of discount airlines. If we'd been trying to sell Piggley Pooh just a couple of years earlier, we wouldn't have been able to get out of Ireland, never mind reach Cannes. Even now as I write this piece, by logging onto the internet, I can book a ticket to Cannes for €11.99 each way from Luton on Easyjet. Thank God for low-cost carriers. The patron saint of the entrepreneur has to be Michael O'Leary, CEO of Ryanair. The fact that Francis had been a year ahead of O'Leary in Clongowes arguably made him more aware of the discount flight possibilities initiated by O'Leary. It undoubtedly ensured that Ryanair was his most used airline.

One of the great problems about being poor is the amount of time it takes. You end up spending hours on saving a euro that you could more profitably spend selling or developing your project.

Looking back, though, Francis glosses over that annoyance. What weighs heavily with him is the time taken away from our children. He remembers the sensation of being thumped amidships when he heard a psychologist on a radio programme pointing out that in this time-poor world most people live in, the young years of your children flash by. He remembers, too, the comment he read to the effect that very few executives, at the end of their lives, say: 'I wish I could have spent more time in the office.' Instead, they talk sadly about not spending enough time with their children. Francis, through his commitment to our project, spent so much time away from his children that when he arrived home, I noticed he hugged and cuddled them like a returned emigrant.

As the project moved through 1996, 1997, 1998, 1999 through to the Disney courtcase judgement in 2001, many of our advisors, particularly our accountants, lost faith en route. We started with Mary Leonard of KPMG Corporate Finance and moved then to Colm Nagle at BDO Simpson Xavier. There was no revenue income in sight. Colm was, as was Mary, extremely positive and extremely helpful. Inevitably, though, the long arduous grind, the rejections, the wait, the constant threats and persecution from Disney took its toll. One by one, they ceased to be involved. Yet, every time we thought we'd reached the end, we would find someone else willing to trust us and our dream and to invest time and expertise in both.

A younger accountant, Barry Rothwell, who has a practice on Mount Street, came on board to help with a business plan we submitted to Irish multimillionaire Denis O'Brien. Barry worked with us on the basis that if we won money from Denis O'Brien, Barry would receive a payment.

After the third meeting with O'Brien's people, Francis was particularly excited. He was advised that an investment was being considered and we were asked would we be prepared to part with control of the project. This was a real speedbump for a lawyer like Francis who understood that once you let control pass that the project could be moved in a direction which was not to the creator's liking. Since Francis had to live with the creator of Piggley Pooh – me – this filled him with dread. However we were now desperate. Our banks were no longer funding us. We were horrifically reliant on friends and family and knew we could not continue to exploit them, no matter what confidence we had in the project's eventual success. Our friends and family had children, their own investments and they own worries and while they might be excited by the prospect of a television investment their excitement would necessarily wane as no return on investment seemed to be forthcoming pending resolution of the Disney case.

A fourth meeting happened with the Denis O'Brien people. Then a fifth. Next step, Francis was to meet Denis O'Brien's right hand man, Lesley Buckley, a well-known Irish businessman with a number of successful ventures under his belt. Francis knew this was a special meeting. A make or break encounter. He was now face to face with a business man who could fund and resource this project.

'I can't be sure of your project,' Buckley told him. 'Television is a very risky business. However, anyone who stands up to a major corporation as you and your wife have done deserves support. That's why we are interested.'

Francis came back from the Buckley meeting quite enthused. He had won a 'yes', subject only to William Fry Solicitors in Dublin sanctioning the deal. That meant they would have to do a due diligence. Unfortunately for us, William Frys did a due diligence and advised Lesley Buckley that we could not win our case against Disney. The yes turned, overnight, into a no. Another crushing disappointment.

We tried everything. We went to Enterprise Ireland, which helps to fund start-up and medium-sized businesses. Michael Kenna, a firm supporter of our project from inception in 1996, gave us the princely sum of £3,000 which, at the time, was a king's ransom. In 1997 he sanctioned a £30,000 grant which in real terms was £15,000, contingent as it was on us being able to raise £15,000 ourselves. We couldn't raise it. The grant lapsed.

In our personal financial lives, people to whom we owed money were always generous and understanding when we explained our difficulties. In particular, Orla Shields, my gynaecologist, never demanded payment of her fees and as a result we were always probably two babies behind with our bills. Tommy Mallon, our builder, was owed a final payment for at least a year and was a real gentleman.

Each time something like losing the Enterprise Ireland grant happened, we thought, 'This is it. This is the worst than can befall us.' Each time, we were wrong. Worse could – and did – happen. One Saturday morning, when I was heavily pregnant with George, in November 2000 Klaragh ran into our kitchen in a panic, shouting:

'Daddy, Mammy,' she yelled, 'the police car is here. The police are outside.'

I thought she must be imagining it, having inherited her mother's lively, not to say over-active, imagination. But no. The doorbell rang. Outside was a sergeant from the garda station in Dunshaughlin, our nearest town in Meath.

'Does Denise Fitzpatrick live here?'

The grave tone of the question transfixed me. I stood in total silence while Francis confirmed that I did.

'I'm sorry,' the officer said gently. 'I have a warrant for your arrest for non payment of a tax bill.'

I had to sit down. I couldn't believe what I was hearing – I was to be arrested for non payment of a tax bill and brought to prison. Francis went into overdrive, but very calmly. He first of all suggested that the sergeant have a cup of tea with us and allow Francis time as my lawyer to examine the arrest warrant. The police officer was almost as distressed as I was. He could see that I was so heavily pregnant that the strong arm of the law could cause the baby to arrive on the spot. He agreed that a cup of tea might be a good course of action, in the circumstances.

Francis kept the conversation going with him over tea and biscuits. The guard was a father of four young children and sympathised completely with us and with Francis who said that if I was taken to Mountjoy prison he would not be able to cope with looking after our children alone. Knowing that the sympathy evinced was not going to stand in the way of a garda síochána doing his duty, I sat opposite him at our kitchen table, trembling at the thought that I was going to be arrested and brought to prison.

Francis, meanwhile, read and re-read the summons.

'We have a problem here, officer,' he said soberly. 'There's a defect in this.'

He turned it around to point out that it was addressed to another Denise Fitzpatrick at an address that I had never lived at. Suddenly, Francis was all business. He was able to confirm to the officer and prove it from court documents that he had successfully got three tax warrants against me struck out as, since we had been married and our taxes were jointly assessed, the revenue were incorrect in seeking taxes from me as an individual. The guard, as relieved, I suspect, as I was, noted the details, apologised for taking our time, shook hands with us and headed off in the squad car.

It was a half an hour before I could get the strength together to stand up and head for our bedroom.

'It can't get any worse than today,' Francis said, his hand warm on my back.

I leaned into him. Hoping he was right. Fearful that he might not be.

Chapter Thirteen

POKING THE 800 POUND GORILLA WITH A STICK

Poor Piggley Pooh. Everybody loved him. They just had a commitment problem. The BBC thought he was delightful. Mondo, an Italian company, were champing at the bit to get him on screen. Public Broadcasting Service in the US were eager to beam him into fifty million homes. But the prospect of having to face down Disney in court over our pig's surname cooled their urgency. They didn't quite say 'See you when the litigation is over and you've won, not that you will', but that's what they meant.

'Get out of it somehow,' Ricky from Mondo advised us. 'Change the name. Call the pig something else. Call him anything else.'

Another suggestion was that we should take the 'h' off the end of the second name and call our character Piggley Poo. (This particular suggestion didn't come from an Irish person, who would know that in Ireland, the word 'poo' is a child's term for shit. It would be hard to imagine anything less appropriate.)

I wouldn't hear of removing the 'h' and was livid at the notion that my character could be called by any old name. I hadn't picked Piggley Pooh out of the air. It was the right name, the name a child would pick – the name a child had picked. It represented a strand of my childhood, a link with the idyllic life I had prior to school.

To others who weren't as close to the creation of a character, it wasn't a big issue. To me, it was outrageous for a big corporation to come the heavy on two people because of four letters in a completely different name to their character. They were accusing two innocent people of trying it on and refusing to listen to the truth, which was that my character had come out of my imagination decades before anybody thought it could be animated or that we might make money out of it.

But – more to the point – I couldn't see the character as anything but Piggley Pooh. It was like saying to the original Walt Disney: 'OK, I know you're fond of Mickey as a name for this big-eared mouse, but Maurice will do just as well.' Names matter, I would say fiercely, picking up Klaragh's toys around the house. Klaragh. Not Clara. Names matter because they're central to an identity. It drives me nuts when people call Francis 'Frank'. He isn't Frank. He's Francis, and nobody has the right to re-name him.

I thought I was strong and principled. I've no doubt some of our potential production partners thought me naïve and obstinate, as the months dragged on and the two of us fought to keep our lives – and Piggley – afloat. Francis would spend his days doing conveyancing, snatching time now and then to go to meetings with our trademark agents. Peter McLachlan was doing the bulk of the work, consulting constantly with his father. The two of them were up against Frank B. Dehn and Partners, a major London firm of trademark agents Disney use. It was a war of attrition.

Slow, laborious Disney would send in their objections to us registering Piggley Pooh and they'd say something to the effect that 'Disney have owned this character since they bought it from the A. A. Milne estate. Disney have spent millions developing the character, sales of books in the UK and Ireland, sales of videos, sales of television. Here is a clear attempt by Francis Fitzpatrick to steal their copyright, their good name and their reputation.' (Francis got to be the star of the litigation because it was simpler for him to stay on top of all of the data, rather than having to come back to me to check details all of the time, as would have happened if we were both named.) In addition he had, of necessity, to understand his case inside out and he spent every waking hour reading up and studying Intellectual Property law.

We would respond by saying: 'This character was invented by a three-year-old girl on the hill of Tara, County Meath, Ireland and she associated the word commonly used colloquially in Ireland for a strong smell with her grandmother's pigs. This little girl had a favourite pig she named Piggley Pooh.'

This must have been mind-blowing stuff for Disney. Instead of high-flown legal counter-argument, we were saying 'We didn't steal your reputation because you don't have a reputation in Piggley Pooh, he's ours.' We were saying it in the simplest possible way, because Francis kept in mind that the person who would eventually make a decision on the issue was a judge.

'Remember, a judge is a human being,' he would say to me. 'If you can touch that human being, it's very difficult for him or her or them to rule against you.'

So these envelopes stuffed with formal accusations against the two of us kept arriving from Disney, with long, intimidating silences in between, and envelopes stuffed with details about my inner life as a child in Meath kept bouncing back across the Irish Sea to their legal representatives in London, and – no doubt – bouncing from there across the Atlantic to beautiful downtown Burbank, the headquarters of the Disney corporation.

If either Francis or I had actually stopped the mad progress of what we were engaged in, we'd have found ourselves looking over an abyss. We had a character who wasn't worth a penny to us. We were sinking deeper into debt, some of that debt mortifyingly due to our friends. The only people who had the smallest interest in our Piggley were the Disney folk, whose only interest lay in strangling him pre-birth or amputating his surname.

We should have been unhappy, me and Francis. We should have been at each other's throats. We weren't, though. Francis maintains we were happy because we decided to be.

That's one way of looking at it. Another is to say that with the wonderful distraction of a growing family and the equally powerful influence of a strong faith, it wasn't that difficult for us to be happy, particularly since we're both optimists.

You'd expect us to be optimists, since both of us are instinctive salespeople, and good salespeople tend to be optimists. A psychologist named Seligman some years ago went through the CVs of a bunch of people who had failed to get jobs as sales representatives with an insurance company in the US called MetLife and picked out the ones who scored highly on optimism. He asked MetLife, as an experiment, to employ this group of rejects for a year and to measure their performance against the people MetLife had chosen to hire instead of them. At the end of that first year, the optimistic 'rejects' had outsold the regular sales corps by twenty-one per cent. MetLife, intrigued, kept the thing going, and found the trend reinforced in the second year, when the optimists outdid the rest by fifty-one per cent.

What Seligman found makes perfect sense to me. I'm a chronic optimist. I'm not stupid. I'm not unrealistic. I take cognisance of all negative possibilities. But I think that you can do anything if you set your mind to it. People limit themselves and then blame other people or circumstances when they don't achieve their hopes and dreams.

We went through bad times over Piggley Pooh, but even on the worse days those bad times didn't compare with the suffering people experience when, for example, they have a child with a serious disability. Francis feels the same. I remember him showing me a cutting about a woman with major spinal disease, who suffered pain so excruciating that only constant injected morphine could reach it.

'Compared to her, our problems are nothing,' Francis said. 'Imagine that pain. Against that, who are Disney? They can't really affect the two of us in any real fundamental way.'

It was quite difficult to explain to those close to us why we weren't distraught. The situation was alarming to our parents. Francis' dad had achieved a fabulous career. At one stage he was overseas controller of the Hong Kong Bank, and was able to send all his eight children to boarding school. The family, because of Mr Fitzpatrick's position, lived a very privileged life in India and Pakistan and Hong Kong. Stability and a strong career path had worked so beautifully for his parents, they naturally worried about the instability and risk of the route he was taking. His father was generously lending him money, but inevitably worrying that Francis and I might be jeopardising the future education of our children out of selfishness and a mad addiction to an impossible project. Francis eventually had to say to his parents that if they didn't stop telling him to give up the Disney case, he was going to stop visiting them because they were upsetting and frightening him.

Francis worked hard – for the children's sake – at being easy and good-humoured. Klaragh had been joined in December 1998 by Daniel, our first-born son. George was to arrive in July 2001 and Patrick in August 2002. Molly arrived in March 2004. In spite of the work he had to do, and his frequent trips abroad, Francis managed to spend more time with his children than did many of his legal colleagues. It was nothing for him to have his work done by noon in order to collect the kids and spend the afternoon in Bushy Park or bring them down to his parents. He yearned to spend as much time as possible with them: 'If you start chasing the dollar or mammon, you ain't going to be happy,' Francis says. 'You have to focus on your children, and when you do, they help you solve your business problems. They're stress busters. To mind our toddlers for two hours allowed me to find work actually easy.'

It helped that finally, in 2000, we had a home. After our initial problems about getting planning permission, we had eventually managed to build Bramblewood House: 4,000 square feet of beautifully designed home on the hill of Skryne where the Celtic soul lives. The hill that we live on is known as Cnoc na Quilla in Irish, meaning 'The Weeping Hill'. After a rebellion of the Fianna army in Tara, King Cormac Mc-Art's son, Cabhra, was sent over to quell the rebellion but, in the process, was fatally wounded. As he lay dying, word reached Tara that his wife should come immediately. She arrived just as he was taking his final breath and started keening. Hence the weeping hill.

The field where we built the house is famous, too, because the Hill of Skryne had the largest annual fair in Leinster up to the famine. After the famine it was reincarnated and it survived up to the 1920s. The British army used to buy most of the horses for export at the Skryne Fair and they would tether the horses in our four and a half acres. Many of those horses went to India and Pakistan – just as Francis had done before coming back to live in Ireland as a little boy.

Family life was brilliant. But in our work life – with the exception of the Piggley Pooh shop in St Stephen's Green – we were just surviving from one crisis to another, and trying to take seriously what, on the face of it, was so ridiculous as to be funny. My big lawyer husband was driving off each day to meet other, more specialist trademark agents and lawyers, to address the individuality of something that didn't exist, and bringing me home the paperwork documenting his case against Disney.

'He stated that the respective characters are entirely different,' one of the documents read. 'His character (our character, I thought possessively) is a fully grown pig, wearing spectacles and reading a book. As such ... it is completely different from the bear named Winnie the Pooh ... a visual comparison of the two characters would confirm that there could be no reasonable basis for suggesting that confusion might occur between the two.'

Not only did we have to argue for the uniqueness of Piggley based on his specs and reading matter, we also had to get into his social life, to establish that 'although Winnie the Pooh may have a "friend" called Piglet it should be noted that a piglet is a young pig and that ... Piggley Pooh refers only to [a] unique adult pig character.'

All of this seemed like daft make-work to me. Boiled down to its essence, my view was that Disney had an idea that we were going to coat-tail on their *Winnie the Pooh* success in order to make money out of Piggley Pooh. The association of a one-syllable word was, in some strange way, going to cast a commercial glow all over my pig so that people fell over themselves wanting to buy him. Oh, right. The word 'Pooh' as a modern version of 'Open Sesame'. If that was the case, then TV stations around the world would long ago have beaten a path to our home in Skryne to buy the rights to my storytelling pig.

Such an association, even if it had been intended, would have been counter-productive. Let's assume someone, seduced by the magic monosyllable 'Pooh' tuned in to our programme, believing it to be some kind of line-extension of Winnie the Pooh. Within thirty seconds, they would know they were in the wrong country – literally.

Winnie the Pooh is set in an idealised Victorian English countryside. Piggley Pooh is set in a working farm in Ireland. Winnie the Pooh's stories are told by an unseen observer.

Piggley Pooh's stories, on the other hand, are told by Piggley himself, and carry a strong resonance of the seanchaí, the storyteller-by-the-open-fire associated with the strongly oral folk-culture in Ireland. So if a fan of Winnie the Pooh managed to mislead themselves into watching Piggley Pooh, the misapprehension, far from being an advantage to our product, would be a distinct disadvantage: they would be getting something so different to what they wanted that they could only be discontented.

Page after page was added to our submission. It wasn't just that Piggley had specs and a book, it was that the 'pooh' in his name, as Francis pointed out, is a dictionary word habitually used by children well before its adoption as part of the name Winnie the Pooh. Hmm, I thought, reading this. *So who says you, Disney, even own the word 'Pooh'? If it was in common use before A. A. Milne started using it, maybe you don't have copyright on it, either.*

Meanwhile, the corporation dedicated to producing wholesome charming entertainment for children were coming right back at us like an 800 pound gorilla. They were swamping us with legal paper, some of which implied that Milne books were to be found in the Meath area when I was growing up and that *Winnie the Pooh* had appeared on television at that time. All of this was funded by a big company to establish the likelihood that I had read about or seen Winnie the Pooh and developed a cunning plan to steal him and morph him into a pig. When I was six. Or maybe seven.

We were fighting back with everything we owned – and a lot of money we didn't own.

It was only afterward that it struck us how irritating it must have been for Steve Ackerman, the Disney executive in charge of legal affairs, when he got letters from Francis with our drawing of Piggley Pooh up on the left hand side as a logo, with the name written large in whimsical lettering. It never occurred to us to use anything else – not that we had the money to develop alternative letter-heads.

Without even meaning to, we were poking the 800 pound gorilla with a sharp stick.

Chapter Fourteen

BEAUTIFUL DOWNTOWN BURBANK

When you're new to the business of poking the 800 pound gorilla with a sharp stick, there's a certain excitement to it: David and Goliath. But you anticipate – or at least I anticipated – that the gorilla would rise up and smite us mightily. Or at least speedily.

It took a resentful while for me to learn that an 800 pound gorilla has a thick skin and time on its hands. It knows it's the biggest threat around, so it doesn't have to rush into anything. In fact, it has an investment in not rushing into anything. The longer it lies dormant, making like it's hibernating, the better it conserves its strength, while its pint-sized opponent is exhausting its energies long before the real battle begins.

As winter turned to spring in 2000, Francis, too was aching for this Disney thing to come to a head. Or a conclusion. Or a bloody good fight. Because Francis knew that Disney was out to strangle the marketing prospects of the tiny annoyance in Ireland, while forcing it to spend money it didn't have on lengthy legal responses to an endless stream of paperwork.

While the gorilla slept, the Fitzpatricks were welcome to run around its 800 pound bulk and exhaust their little selves, not to mention their money and their chances of ever turning their pig into a household name. If the gorilla ever woke, the Fitzpatricks would be older, weaker, poorer and perhaps – from the gorilla's point of view – wiser. They would certainly have less fight in them.

Then one day, Francis arrived home and flung his briefcase on the table. It was like the old film instructions: Lights, Camera – Action! We mightn't have lights or camera, but Francis was definitely going to deliver the action. At least in our kitchen.

'We're not taking this anymore,' he announced.

'Not taking what anymore?'

'This General Patton stuff.'

For a mad moment, I thought Francis must have a client named General Patton who was giving him a hard time. He then explained that General Patton had been a Second World War leader on the allied side, and an aggressive manager of men, material and matters legal. According to Francis, the General Patton theory of war was 'Make the bastards spend all their money and then kill them'.

'That's what's behind all this Disney delay,' he said. 'They're just trying to bleed us dry, to exhaust us so we'll go away. Or be easily killed off, like Patton says. To hell with that. I'm not taking it anymore. I've asked Norman to contact Frank B. Dehn in London and set up a meeting in Burbank.'

'So?' I asked, tidying the thrown briefcase off the table.

'What do you mean, "so"?' Francis asked. 'You've been nagging for something to happen –'

I opened my mouth to deny nagging, then closed it again.

'Now, I've *made* something happen,' he said, severely, taking the briefcase back, I thought, for another throw. 'In *Burbank*.'

Before I could stop myself, I could feel my shoulders coming up in a 'so what?' shrug.

'What'll you gain by talking to these guys in London that you haven't already covered by writing to them?'

Francis set down the briefcase and gave me a quick lesson in *dramatis personae* and geography. For a starter, he was not going to meet the minions, he was going to meet the big boys. Forget Frank B. Dehn, he was going to talk directly to Steve Ackerman. This, I thought, is progress. And furthermore, Francis said, Burbank was an important suburb of Hollywood.

'I've never heard of it,' I said.

'"Beautiful downtown Burbank" used to be the opening line of the *Laugh-in*,' Francis said.

'What's the *Laugh-in*?' I asked, only half-joking.

'TV programme Goldie Hawn started on.'

'Way before my time,' I said. 'So we're bound for Burbank?'

Francis nodded.

'How soon?'

Francis shook his head: dunno.

'When's the appointment?'

Another headshake.

'You do *have* an appointment?'

By now, Francis was beginning to look like those little figurines where the heads nod (or shake from side to side) forever. He didn't have an appointment, he explained, because he didn't have the assent of Disney to his proposed plan of action. He had, however, got decisive with Frank B. Dehn, demanding that such an appointment be set up.

'But if you're going to ask me do I think they'll come back quickly with a date,' he said, fending me off. 'The answer is I doubt it.'

'More postponement?'

'More postponement.'

Francis was now sitting in the kitchen, looking more and more disconsolate as he realised my interpretation of his big advance was that it had merely delivered us another slice of delay.

'Listen, at least they know you're a strong guy who's not

prepared to sit on your ass letting them ignore you,' I said, trying to retrieve things.

'No, they'll probably think I'm even weaker as a result,' Francis said. (When Francis gets disconsolate, which he doesn't frequently, he gets seriously disconsolate.)

'How could they think you were weaker?'

'They'll figure we are running out of money and are desperate. So desperate that we're prepared to fly over there on our own money and seek an audience with them. But the reality is that if we don't take action now, we're going to be so far in the debt hole, we won't be able to afford to buy a ticket to go out there.'

'Did Norman say that to them?'

'No, Norman put it in the best possible light, saying that his client, Francis Fitzpatrick was amenable to a suggestion coming from Norman that a face-to-face meeting might allow the matters between us to be resolved. Amicably. But how soon – if at all – Disney in the US will respond, God knows. When you're dealing with corporate behemoths, a month is a short space of time.'

I nodded, trying to be serious, but a giggle fought its way out of me. Francis looked surprised.

'I'm sorry,' I said. 'But there's something weird about the two of us at the kitchen table agreeing that a month is a short space of time for a corporate – what was it you called them again?'

'A behemoth.'

'What the hell is a behemoth?' (Having not known where Burbank was, I wasn't going to try to pretend intimate knowledge of behemoths ...)

'A hairy mammoth, I think.'

'What's a – Oh, never mind. Disney, the hairy mammal, are going –'

'Moth.'

'What?'

'Hairy mamMOTH.'

'Disney, the hairy mammoth, are going to take several years to answer Norman because that's what behemoths do.'

As it turned out, though, this particular behemoth must have been going through a speedy period. Within a month, it sent word back that a meeting with Francis at their studio HQ would be OK. It didn't say it was the happiest woolly mammoth alive, just thinking about meeting Francis, but it was a civil enough response, and we packed our bags. That is, we packed our bags after I had insisted that Francis went to *Boutique Homme* in South Anne Street and bought himself a new suit together with a couple of shirts and ties. Battling a behemoth required a bit of power dressing, I told him. He came home with a stunning dark Valentino that cost enough to house a small family for a year.

'I told the assistant that I was going to America to fight for my life,' Francis explained, laying it all out. 'So he threw in a tie for free.'

'For free?' I asked, solemnly.

Francis got red and laughed: 'The guy knew I really needed a free tie.'

'What a shame I won't be going to the meeting with you,' I said, deadpan. 'I might have got a free handbag along with my new suit. Maybe a Fendi.'

The suit got packed, along with the free tie, and Klaragh and Daniel were handed over to my mum and dad. It's a funny thing about leaving your children when they're very young. They're not the smallest bit sad, because they're going to their grandparents' house, where they're guaranteed they'll be spoiled rotten. The grandparents are not sad, because they're going to be in total control for a little while, having the chance to correct all the things they believe the parents are doing wrong. And the parents, while they dread

191

the absence, still have a sneaky pleasure at the thought of a few nights of blissfully uninterrupted sleep. It's a great deal, all round.

Flying to New York with Aer Lingus was no problem. Flying on to San Francisco was no problem. The problem was San Francisco to Burbank. Although Francis at least knew where Burbank was, he didn't know that San Francisco, like Cork Airport, is subject to godawful fog, which delayed the connecting flight. The two of us were there on time, ready for the final leg of the long journey, but was the plane ready to transport us there? No. Instead, the notice on the board said there would be a delay. Then it said there would be another delay. Then it added a further hour to the second delay.

Francis went to the check-in desk. He was not alone. An enormous crowd milled around in front of the sign that had changed from 'on time' to 'delayed'. Half the world seemed to have tickets to Burbank that night. For all the good those tickets were doing them. Watching his back as he waited for his chance to talk to the desk clerk, I supplied my own line of argument to him. Not out loud, of course: *Look, most of the families waiting are exhausted. Listen to the children crying. They'd gain from an overnight in a hotel. None of them have a life-or-death urgency about getting to Burbank, but we do.*

He reached the top of the line, and the desk clerk looked up at him with that expression filled with weary courtesy. He nodded gravely as Francis talked. Except that the nods had the same gravity he'd employed on dozens of earlier passengers who had preceded Francis. Francis leaned in towards the guy, mixing urgency with warmth: *I know you understand our problem like nobody else in the world understands it, and that you'll find a way around this fog and get me to my important meeting with the Disney behemoth.*

The weary courtesy stayed on the clerk's face as he began

to respond. By the time Francis struggled out of the crowd around the check-in desk and got back to me, I knew the essence, if not the details, of the clerk's message.

'I appreciate your problem,' went that message. 'I understand your situation. I feel your pain. Right now, there's not a lot I can do about it. But why don't you check back with me at ten and we'll see where we're at, then?'

Our flight was already four hours overdue. When Francis went back at ten, the clerk told him – with an air of achievement – that he could put us on the red-eye. The red-eye? Shorthand for the dawn flight. Leaving at 6 a.m. The extra good news the clerk confided was that United Airlines had negotiated a very special rate for us at the Ramada Inn, where we could stay overnight. It was the first time I'd run into what has turned into a major trend: airlines making you pay for bad weather. In the past, they tended to put you in a hotel and cough up for the delay. Not anymore.

Francis did the best he could to sound appreciative for this special rate, and asked me to wait while he found a public phone. His priority? To cancel the booking at the Holiday Inn in Burbank for that night so we wouldn't end up paying double. I don't imagine the Holiday Inn loved us for ringing them to cancel at 10.30 at night, but they were pleasant about it and waived the charge.

That done, off the two of us hiked to the Ramada for an overnight that didn't feel like an overnight, given that we were getting into bed just shy of midnight, and had to be up again just after four. Francis likes to go to sleep with the television on. I hate having the TV on when I'm trying to go to sleep. In this case, though, I told him he was welcome to the TV. He was going to need all the sleep he could stuff into the four hours in the Ramada.

Next morning, the flight to Burbank took fifty minutes. Fifty easy minutes with dawn coming in the windows. You couldn't imagine that this tiny journey could have caused such hassle the night before.

'Isn't this a glorious morning?' Francis enthused, coming out of the airport. 'Wouldn't you be glad to be alive?'

Not if I was you, I thought silently. *Not if I was headed for a battle with the massed legal brains of the behemoth, all of whom will be well-slept, while you've had four hours of fitful slumber.* I kept this to myself, enthusing obediently about California's wonderful mornings.

The meeting was due at eleven, so at 10.30, Francis, in full Valentino, demanded a final check-over by me. I turned him around and admired him from every angle, trying to be both calm and funny about it.

'What are you worried about?' I asked rhetorically. (Answer: bankruptcy, failure, poverty, disaster. To name but a few.)

'Who says I'm worried?' he asked rhetorically.

'It's going to be easy peasy,' I said, patting him on the back. But gently, for fear he'd shatter.

''Course it is,' he said, hugging me so tight I thought *I'd* shatter.

Then he was gone and I was left alone. A couple of hours later, that Holiday Inn bedroom would have won first prize in a worldwide contest for the tidiest hotel room in captivity.

Meanwhile, Francis was sitting in a taxi demolishing his own confidence by asking himself why the hell he was doing this on his own, given that the first rule of litigation is: don't do it for yourself. While the pastel buildings of Burbank flashed by the windows of the cab, two voices in his head started an argument about his situation.

'You could have taken any one of your brilliant legal friends and contacts with you. Why the hell didn't you?'

'Because I couldn't afford to pay them.'

194

'That hasn't stopped you getting help from them back home.'

'Because I couldn't afford to pay for their flight.'

'That didn't stop you and Denise coming out.'

In desperation, he took out his rosary beads and started to quietly recite the rosary to himself. If the taximan noticed that this big Valentino-clad Irishman was working his way through prayer-beads, he had the wit to be silent about it.

Francis finished the rosary. As he was stuffing the beads back into his pocket, he suddenly recalled something an old neighbour of mine said to us, the day I introduced her to my new fiancé: 'Always remember,' Agnes Hughes had said, sitting by the fire in my parents' home, 'always remember that, together, the two of you can achieve anything.'

Once at the right building, Francis gave Steve Ackerman's name and was brought to a boardroom, congratulating himself on his punctuality. Here he was, right on the button of his appointed time, all on his own in a massive boardroom, waiting for Steve Ackerman, who, he was assured, would be along 'presently'. OK, Francis thought. Big guy like Steve Ackerman will want to impress on a small guy like Francis Fitzpatrick just how teeny he is, so he'll let him simmer for about ten minutes before he appears. Francis was comfortable enough with that trick, and set out to explore the big boardroom. 'Big' didn't begin to describe the place. Forty large comfortable chairs surrounded the table.

Francis picked what he believed would be the best location within this vast terrain. He pulled out the little DVD recorder on which he planned to play them his pilot video. This demonstration would, he told himself, instantly convince them that there was no possible connection between their red t-shirted bear and our waistcoated seanchaí pig.

After ten minutes, there was action. Of a sort. A waiter arrived with drinks. Francis chose lemonade. Sipping it, he remembered stories he had been told about the early years of the Pepsi and Coca-Cola territory wars, when successful salesmen from one of the competing companies would be found dead in ditches, allegedly done in by rival salesman intent on signing up the territory and making huge commissions. His mouth curled around the lemonade, which had come out of an open, iced jug. Disney might have an external image that was warm and cuddly, but its founder hadn't been that warm and cuddly in his private life, and we hadn't found the corporation that pleasant to deal with thus far. Who knew how far they were prepared to go to take out a competitor who might dent the billions they make every year from A. A. Milne's little bear?

Francis poured the lemonade into the base of a potted plant. If it was going to poison anything, let it poison a plant. He looked at the plant for a minute to see how it was doing. It didn't look like it was going through the throes of cyanide-ingestion, but then he realised it was made of silk, which probably wasn't going to be affected by cyanide. He rinsed out the glass with fresh lemonade from a can, believing that not even Disney would have poisoned a drink inside a can, and drank the rest of the canned lemonade.

He had time for two or three more drinks, as it turned out, because the room continued to be a bleak business cavern, chilled by a whispering air conditioner, and occupied by Francis alone, for ten more minutes, then another ten, then a further ten. He decided against opening any of the remaining drinks, however, on the basis that if he drank them, he would be dying to go to the loo, which would unman him in the coming confrontation with Steve Ackerman. Indeed, he decided, now flying high on waves of paranoia, that was probably the cunning plan behind leaving him in this big empty room with nothing but beverages.

Of course, he then thought, they have this room bugged.

Not just bugged with microphones, but probably bugged with hidden cameras, to give Ackerman advance information on the frame of mind of those with whom he negotiates. Francis decided he had to send body-language signals to the hidden cameras, although he was somewhat hampered by not knowing where exactly they might be. But he walked confidently around the room a lot, smiling to himself as if at pleasant memories, glancing out the window in what he hoped was a bored but not tense way.

If Steve Ackerman enjoyed this show or had access to it, he didn't say when he eventually arrived in the room, accompanied by his assistant, Heidi Stromberg. He bounced in, all enthusiasm, no apologies, forty minutes after the meeting had been scheduled to start, a tall, balding, well-built man with glasses. How had Francis' flight been? Francis told him. Ackerman was all sympathy over the airport's propensity to fog up.

The two men exchanged bits of personal background. Ackerman had been first a lawyer in New York, then an entertainment specialist, and finally joined Disney as its chief counsel worldwide. Francis glanced at Heidi. Personal details? Forget it. If she had any, they weren't going to be shared. She was there to take notes and notes she was going to take.

'We got us a problem here, Francis,' Ackerman said, cutting to the chase.

The problem, he stated, was one of theft. We had stolen a name that belonged to his people. Two names. Pooh and Piglet. We'd marginally altered Piglet, juxtaposed it with Pooh, and hoped to make millions as a result.

'You won't get away with it,' he said flatly.

Francis forced himself to stay calm – no easy task when you're being called a thief by someone who isn't trying to conceal their contempt for you. He talked about my childhood and how, without any immersion in A. A. Milne's work, I had taken a word commonly used to register a smell, and applied it in a childlike way to a pet pig which had later become a character in stories. Ackerman heard him out. Just about.

'Look, we have the resources to prove that *Winnie the Pooh* was around in Ireland when your wife was growing up,' he said. 'Consciously or unconsciously, she stole the name. *Nobody* is going to believe she invented it. Nobody. The theft is too obvious.'

Francis got launched on Irish usage and on the sort of cultural influences that formed my references and ideas. Ackerman quickly tired of this.

'Oh, come *on*,' he said, his tone inviting Francis to confess malfeasance. 'You stole it, you Irish bastard.'

Francis goggled at him, astonished by the sudden descent into personal abuse. He had envisaged that the Disney people might employ all sorts of intimidatory negotiation tactics, but calling their opponent an Irish bastard hadn't presented itself as a real and present possibility. Ackerman leaned forward.

'Listen, Francis,' he said, his eyes hard as slate. 'You're not gonna get the better of the Disney corporation. *Nobody* gets the better of Disney. We got the resources. We got the time. We got right on our side. We'll go after you all around the world and bankrupt you. You're a family man. You got children. You need to think again.'

Francis was chilled by the tone of the threat. He began to flounder. To talk about there being no point in continuing these discussions, that perhaps seeing each other in court was the only way to go. This, he thought, is how a hare feels when it's being coursed.

Ackerman cut through what Francis was saying.

'You're an attorney,' he snapped. 'You should know you got no chance of winning.'

That, Francis mentally admitted, was probably true. He was, after all, sitting in this very office because he doubted that a married couple from Meath could take on a multinational entertainment giant. Ackerman sighed, shaking his head in wonderment at Francis' foolishness. Heidi Stromberg's pen halted, briefly. She couldn't make notes of a headshake.

'You got young *children*,' he murmured. 'You and your wife have got to look after them, not waste their future …'

Wrong button to press. I could have told him that, if I'd been there. To suggest to Francis that his children are not his first and final priority is a big mistake. Huge. Up to now, Francis had been confused, intimidated, unclear as to where to start tackling the issues raised. The first mention of our children by Ackerman Francis had registered but not reacted to. The second one put him into orbit. Francis didn't just see red. He saw every colour in the rainbow.

'Don't you threaten my children,' he yelled at Ackerman. 'Don't you even *mention* my children. Ever again.'

Once the cork was out of the Francis bottle, everything inside came out in a wild torrent of verbal abuse delivered at the top of Francis' voice. Disney's worldwide counsel got descriptions of his morals, origin and motivation lashed at him, held together with a clump of four-letter words. Heidi Stromberg gazed at Francis as if he was a nuclear power station going through meltdown. He had a mad urge to tell her to concentrate on what she was doing and make notes of every insult he had thrown at her boss.

'If we're talking thieves,' Francis continued, now past all discretion or judgement. 'Disney is the king of thieves. My God, you people want to steal a dream, you want to steal something that's been part of my wife's childhood since she was a toddler, you want to steal our rights to tell stories in the way generations of Irish seanchaí have told stories – of wisdom and challenge and battles and beauty. Well, why don't we do it the other way? Why don't I buy your Winnie the Effing Pooh instead?'

The daftness of this last proposal may have been apparent to Ackerman, but even he couldn't have known just how daft it was, coming from a man who had gone rushing to a phone the night before to avoid having to pay two separate hotel bills. Ackerman didn't get into discussion of the daft offer, however, possibly distracted by hearing the character he was sworn to defend described as Winnie the Effing Pooh. He took off his glasses, polished them, and put them back on again. Heidi Stromberg sat as still as if she'd been turned to stone. A long silence fell. Francis was thirsty after his outburst, but he wasn't going to be seen by Ackerman to need a drink, so he sat there, dusty-mouthed and still boiling with fury over our children being brought into a business discussion. Particularly by a lawyer representing a corporation whose mega-billions had all been earned through children and which – supposedly – held strong family values.

'Francis, you've achieved a hell of a lot,' Ackerman said slowly, his voice newly soft. Oh, right, Francis thought. Here comes the love-bomb.

'We really didn't expect you and your wife –'

'Denise,' Francis said.

'We really didn't expect you and Denise to come this far.'

I'll bet you didn't, Francis thought. But then, you haven't met Denise yet. When you do, *if* you do, you'll begin to understand why attacking my family is the wrong way to go.

'You're still fighting us in litigation,' Ackerman went on. 'That's a credit to you.'

This slightly confused Francis, who was so constantly juggling credit cards that he thought at first it was a reference to money. It took him a second to realise he was being praised for perseverance.

'You really must consider finding a resolution that will accommodate Disney and accommodate your own needs. Let's try and be gentlemen. Let's try and find a win/win solution.'

He began to shuffle paper around on the big table. Locating what he was looking for, he addressed the issue of the US trademark. Francis dealt with that issue at some length. They moved on to the Japanese trademark. On that, Francis was equally expert. Ackerman and Fitzpatrick: talking across an over-sized boardroom table with an over-paid note-taker acting as stenographer. One bit of Francis' mind was observing the process and registering, for the first time, how very competent he had become on international intellectual property rights law. Nothing Ackerman raised was outside his understanding.

They got to the looming courtcase in what was now shaping up to become the European theatre of war between the two sides. Any time Ackerman upped the pace, or came close to re-visiting accusations of theft, Francis simply repeated his proposal that he buy out Disney's *Winnie the Pooh*. It was the antithesis to win/win negotiation practice, but it worked, every time. It worked because it reduced Ackerman to a few moments of maddened silence, during which time Francis re-grouped and took the discussion somewhere else.

Hours into the argument – because it was still an argument – Ackerman gathered his papers together and suggested Francis come back to him with a 'realistic proposal' for settling the case. Floating in the air, but never quite stated, was the indication that Disney would look favourably on paying us a sum that would obviate their having to go to the trouble and expense of killing us in the courts of Europe, Japan and the US. While they would undoubtedly win in all of these territories, they would consider some minor payment to the Irish pair who were so irrationally determined not to see reason. Unstated but inescapable was the message: you two have nuisance value. Put a reasonable cost on that nuisance value and we'll give it to you to go away.

'That makes sense to me,' Francis said, matching the weary restraint of Ackerman's tone. 'I'll go away and do precisely as you suggest. I'll be able to do it quickly, too, because I know that the minimum monetary settlement I could reasonably accept to compensate me for five years of working with the trademark and building up the reputation of the Piggley Pooh offering is $20,000,000.'

Heidi Stromberg went back to stone statue mode. Steve Ackerman closed his eyes in disbelief. *This* was where they had got to after several hours of hard work?

'Of course, that doesn't address at all Denise's creative input, and I can't speak for how she would feel about it,' Francis added. 'But I'll get back to you very quickly on this, we want closure and I know you do, too.'

Ackerman opened his mouth, no doubt to establish that while he wanted closure, he didn't want it badly enough to hand over twenty million smackers.

Before he could say anything, though, Francis was on his feet, all good humour, holding out a wooden gift box. It contained Midleton aged Irish whiskey, bought at the duty-free shop in Dublin Airport as a gift for Ackerman. Ackerman smiled stiffly, but didn't put out his hands to take it.

'I thank you for your thoughtfulness,' he said, formally, getting to his feet. 'But I could not accept such a ... gift. Disney has certain rules.'

He swept out the door, trailed by Stromberg. Francis looked at the wooden box in his hands, trying to figure out what Ackerman meant about Disney having 'certain rules'. Then it hit him. Ackerman thought the whiskey was a bribe. Francis started to laugh. Then he remembered the hidden cameras. If there were hidden cameras.

'I don't steal,' he told the Midleton box, sliding it back into the double plastic bag he'd used to carry it in. 'And I don't bribe. But there's no limits to how far I'll go for my wife and family.'

Chapter Fifteen

STEALTH BOMBERS AND KINKO'S

The great thing about *not* going with Francis to a meeting is that he has an almost photographic memory. So, when he came back from the Disney headquarters, I got a blow-by-blow account of what had happened in the huge boardroom, with minor interruptions, like when he stripped off the Valentino suit of armour and headed for the shower.

By the time he reached the point where he had offered the Midleton whiskey and had it rejected, it was evening, and, by now casually dressed, the two of us went out to dinner. Our ravenous hunger made us forget that we were in America, the home of the supersize meal and so, in addition to our main course, we picked side orders of onion rings and mushrooms. The amount of food arriving out on one of those huge round wooden trays, all of it meant for our table, was positively scary. The two of us wanted to say 'take it all back, please'. There was enough for six Irish people. We were embarrassed before we even noticed another table close by with a family who between them hadn't half as much as we had.

Once we got going, though, we made some inroads into that food, and it couldn't have tasted better. I had steak, which may have been hormoned to the last, but was delicious. Francis had something vegetarian and a beer, which may have helped him relax after an unusually stressful day. I was getting high on sugar. Attracted by the picture of one of the cocktails – a pink one with a great deal of alcohol, colour, paper parasols and crushed ice in it, I ordered one. By the end of the meal we were in much better humour. We might not have persuaded Disney to back off their persecution of us, but they now knew what we were like when roused, and they had to be clearer on just how strongly we felt that we were in the right about Piggley Pooh. We were never going to be convinced that 'Pooh' belonged to them, and we were never going to give up.

Knowing we were going to spend the next week with Francis' younger brother, Seán, in Florida, also put the Burbank meeting into perspective. Seán was actually working in Disney. In one of those situations where fact is stranger than fiction. He and his girlfriend, Amy (who he later married), both worked for Disney for a while, although Amy had just given up her Disney post and gone into real estate. Seán, however, was still working for Disney in Pleasure Island in the Orlando resort. Pleasure Island is the adults' playground with drinks, live bands, casinos and game shows.

Heading for Orlando after the meeting in Burbank, from my point of view, was a promise of pure pleasure. Amy was a brilliant person to go shopping with because, as an American, she knew all the best outlet malls where there would be discount branches of stores like Sachs Fifth Avenue and Anne Taylor. Discount branches, plus the weakness of the dollar, meant everything was great value and would allow us, no matter how broke we were, to get some clothing for the kids.

Francis was looking forward to the break because he always enjoyed being with his brother and Amy. We stayed with them for about three days and then decided to spend a few days by the sea. We wanted peace and quiet and recreation, we told the travel agent. No pressure of any kind.

Did she check the dates of other events likely to be going on at the same time? We seriously doubt it. Because she sent us to Fort Lauderdale to the Pelican Beach resort during the noisiest time in the entire calendar: it was the US army military show. The skies were full of jets and stealth bombers for the entire weekend. Ten minutes of it would pierce your eardrums. It was unbelievable. The bellowing of the war planes made *Saving Private Ryan* sound quiet. And the crowds! Everybody in America seemed to have come to Fort Lauderdale for the airshow.

There were planes outside the window of our apartment, on our piece of sand, and there was nothing we could do about it. Even inside the apartment we had to keep our palms over our ears. On one occasion when we went out, we saw a stealth bomber. It came in silently but once it had passed overhead, the noise would blow your mind.

For peace and recreation, we had rented an apartment in the middle of American jihad! I heard one commentator say: 'the next plane that you see, you won't be able to hear, but if we had had one of those, there wouldn't have been a second world war. This stealth bomber costs $1bn and would have wiped out the enemy.' In my mind I calculated that Disney could buy six per year on the back of *Winnie the Pooh*. No wonder they had gone to war with us.

It was amazing and, to be fair, it was quite interesting. It was ironic, it was hysterically funny, but it was also a very tense time because Francis wanted to get his proposal back to Disney within three or four days. He worked away on it himself, but then, to process and assemble it into presentable form, he wanted us both to go to one of those Kinko copyshops that are open day and night. Note that 'us'. I couldn't see the urgency. Disney had delayed us for months, why should we now rush to get a document back to them following a meeting where they'd insulted Francis and – effectively – threatened his family? The way I saw it, preparing the report could wait while we relaxed. The way Francis saw it, preparing the report couldn't wait a second. Well, I'm not stopping you, was my attitude. I'll not stand in your way. Off with you. And enjoy the stealth bombers while you're at it.

And so, he would go on his own, but keep coming back and giving out because he got lost. It was one of those places where every road looks the same. There, you see, I would point out. Your concentration is shot. You need some R&R. Postpone the report, what will you lose? There is no need to do it so quickly. There's no *gain* in killing yourself.

But you couldn't knock him off his block once he wanted or decided to get on a task. It is an extremely irritating admirable trait he has. From the beginning of our relationship together a central component of our business philosophy was a sense of urgency, exemplified by a commitment to get the reply straight back to the client as a way of demonstrating efficiency and professionalism. That approach had always been driven by Francis and supported by me, but in the middle of a Fort Lauderdale reeking of jet fuel, trembling with overhead ordinance and alive with vocal patriotism, insisting on getting the damn report back so quickly seemed to me to be taking it to the extreme.

However, eventually, to mollify him, I agreed to go with him to Kinko's, my first introduction to the place. It's well-equipped, incredibly efficient, much in demand, and I hated it. I hated it partly because of the need to be in more than one queue simultaneously. There were queues for the photocopier and if you were in that queue, then you missed your chance of a place in the queue in the laptop area, and so on.

At this point, Francis had become the walking, talking, sulking, sighing definition of personal stress. He was totally pressured by trying to co-ordinate getting the draft of his proposal back from Robert Ryan, who was our lawyer in Ireland, and from McLachlan Donaldson, our trademark agents. Each of them put good stuff into the proposal and transmitted it to Francis by email. But he discovered that he had left some stuff up in his brother's house and so he needed him to email that to him. Then the composite proposal, incorporating all of the changes suggested by a handful of different people, had to go back to each individual to make sure nothing had crept in which was misleading or illegal. It was just a nightmare. If Francis had been in his own office at home in Ireland, it would still have been a complicated task, but it would have generated at most a quarter of the stress it produced in Fort Lauderdale.

Poor Francis tried his best to explain all the complications to me, but – with the jets still thundering overhead and a lot of sunshine going to waste out of doors – I didn't really want to know. Then he'd feel guilty because he was interfering with my tanning time on the beach. The day he finally dragged me down to Kinko's was one of the least happy of our entire marriage. Once I was there, I was so unhelpful that he says he'd have been better off if I hadn't been there at all.

But you know when people talk resentfully about being a cog in a wheel? I felt as if I was a cog *not* in a wheel. I owned no part of the process.

I'd be sitting there, twiddling my thumbs, looking out at the sunshine and the next thing Francis would come flying at me, asking me to go up and ask the man behind the counter for some supplies. I didn't know what the supplies were for or how far they would get us towards my goal, which was getting the hell out of there. Francis was too harried to find time to tell me which bit of what I was doing (or failing to do) fitted into which bit of the overall task, so I seemed to be constantly doing meaningless trivial tasks to which he attached an unreal urgency.

I reacted by lots of sighs and casting my eyes to heaven, which of course made him madder and madder and more silent and less coherent when he was asking me to do something. The other thing I didn't like was what I read when-ever pages from the report passed in front of me. Six pages went on all the time and effort we had spent on Piggley Pooh and how successful it was at Cannes and at NATPE (the television market in Las Vegas) and the deals that we had signed up to and the shops that were open. I was reading this and thinking 'This is all true, but Francis is making us look like a little empire. Why's he doing that?' And grad-ually, I realised that he was setting us up to be bought out.

Now, on the one hand, I knew this was probably the very best option we could hope for, given that Disney would not tolerate a competing character with a name too close to that of their own character, as they saw it, in the marketplace. But to see, on paper, the evidence that we were prepared to kill my pig if Disney paid us enough, put me into a tailspin. I knew it wasn't fair and that Francis had fought an heroic battle in Burbank for a pig he had neither invented nor named. I knew he also felt that if we could get a half-decent sum out of Disney, it would be the same, financially, as get-ting Piggley on cinema screens worldwide.

We would just have one customer – Disney – instead of thousands of customers each paying the price for a single ticket. Selling to one customer called Disney would make life a lot easier. A settlement is a settlement – it would have been nice. Except that, there in Kinko's, I realised that lots of people paying a tiny amount to see a pig character that had animated life in it was a very different proposition to selling that pig to one rich customer who wanted to kill it. If a settlement is a settlement, a dead character is a dead character. If Disney killed off Piggley, he would be dead for all eternity, and all my creativity with it.

Francis had stressed that it wouldn't be dead for all eter-nity, that, on the contrary, there was a chance we could revive Piggley in due course, because Disney had no problem with the concept itself. The idea of an Irish farm and a pig telling Irish stories didn't cut across their interests in any way. If we changed the name, there would be no opposition from them to us doing something with our own pig once a decent interval of time had elapsed.

I don't know much about the history of animated characters, but I don't think many characters have revived having been crushed by the powerhouse of animated entertainment. Watching Francis fighting with the collating machine in Kinko's, I tried to imagine him going back to Cannes, yet again, trying to convince guys who associated him completely with a pig named Pooh, that he had a completely new character who looked just like the last one, and sounded like the last one, and did the same things in the same location as the last one, but was subtly different.

'And what's the key difference, Francis?'

'Well, the key difference is he now has a different name.'

'What was wrong with the Pooh name, Francis?'

'Nothing. It was a good name.'

'It was a *very* good name, Francis. So why have you abandoned it?'

'Well, Disney bought the character.'

'Wow! Disney! Hey, you guys struck it rich! When will we see it onscreen?'

'Never.'

'*Never?*'

'Never. Disney bought Piggley Pooh because he was so good –'

'Yes?'

'They felt they had to kill him.'

'You're kidding me.'

'Because he might damage Winnie the Pooh. But now that they've killed him, we can use him under a different name.'

'Francis?'

'Yes?'

'Tell ya what. Don't call us, we'll call you.'

Why should they have any other reaction?

I could not kid myself – particularly after shopping in Marshalls on a maxed-out credit card – that we were not broke. We were good and broke. We were in an awful cycle of borrow or die. Logically, we had to get something out of Disney and then find a way, after we paid off all our debts, to still have my little farm on television, in a different guise. Except that we had spent so much time and effort on creating Piggley Pooh that the thought of rebranding him was too horrendous to consider. It buckled me at the knees.

Francis, meanwhile, was looking relieved. Obviously Amy had managed to email through whatever documentation he had left in the house she shared with Seán. One half of me was admiring Francis' dedication to duty, but the other half was thinking 'Seán gave you one of these black surfing t-shirts you leave on all the time to prevent sunburn. It looks lovely on you. The two of us should be on the beach and in the sea instead of in this dive making a million photocopies.' At one point, I said I was getting cokes from the vending machine. Did he want one?

'No thank you,' he said. 'I've given up caffeine.'

'What?'

'I've given up caffeine.'

'When?'

'Today.'

'*Today?*'

"Well, yesterday and today.'

'Why?'

He pushed me gently in front of him to the next workstation. I sat down beside him while he laid out his papers.

'Why?' I persisted.

'Why what?' he asked, already preoccupied with the material laid out in front of him.

'Why've you suddenly given up caffeine?'

'I noticed the other day that Ackerman was in very good physical shape.'

'So?'

'It was a very traumatic meeting with Disney.'

'Yeah?'

'A couple of times when Ackerman mentioned our kids, I couldn't actually breathe. I hyperventilated. I felt I wasn't in peak physical condition and I needed to be. It just clicked there and then: caffeine is not good for you, it changes your heart rate, your body is better off without that toxin – ease off on it. This is a long battle. Maybe the Man above was telling me: be prepared, don't let anything go to chance, train hard, get on with it. So the last time I had coffee was that morning before I left for Burbank.'

'But you don't mind if I do?'

'Not at all.'

At this point, the man behind me in the queue for the workstation got aggravated enough to say *he'd* have no problem if I had caffeine. In fact, if I moved myself speedily out of the chair I was occupying to no good purpose other than discussing the demerits of caffeine and let him take it instead, he'd pay for my can of coke. I damn near took him up on the offer, but I was kind of locked into killer glares that day, so I gave him a killer glare instead as I vacated the seat.

Lashing the coins into the vending machine, I thought to myself that if anybody asks me, when we go home, if I had a good time in California and Florida, I'll brain them.

By the time we got out of Kinko's, Francis had lost maybe six pounds in weight and was completely exhausted. He was sleepy from lack of caffeine, but he was also restless because every time he started to relax, he would wonder if one page had been put in the wrong place or a sentence word-processed into the wrong sequence.

There was, at that stage, nothing he could do to fix any problem he identified, but you can't stop your mind rattling over the same tracks it's been rattling over for days.

Chapter Sixteen

DEAR JOHN ...

Back home in Meath, as soon as the Fort Lauderdale tan began to wear off, we started to check the post, every day, if not every hour, to see if anything had come from Steve Ackerman in response to Francis' proposed solution. It took a lot to restrain us from actually phoning Disney and begging them for a reaction, because we had come back to a situation which was worse than the one we had left.

Day after day, Francis went through variations on the same telephone conversation with different bankers: 'Well, you know yourself, we're in negotiations with Disney.'

'Not the issue, Francis. The issue is the money. We need the debt reduced and reduced quickly.'

'But you know the situation –'

'Doesn't matter that *I* know the situation, what matters is that I've got head office on my back.'

You know the old adage about being between a rock and a hard place? That pretty much summed up where we were. The rock was Disney. No point in trying to nag, whinge, complain or kick it. Rocks don't tend to respond to any of the above. The hard place was our financial situation, personified by our bankers.

Of course, to our bankers, we must have seemed just as intransigent as Disney seemed to us. They kept writing to us and telephoning us and getting cheery postponements and promises from Francis, who was now the greatest living expert at feeding bankers the little extra bits of information which comfort them with the notion of onward progress. Just as Disney had us trapped, we, in a sense, had the bankers trapped. Our growing debt was now so large that no individual banker could afford to have us on his bad debt list. Better to leave us as a potential bad debt and stay on our case.

Disney responded in the middle of June, almost six weeks to the day after our meeting in Burbank. Their response was a classic big corporation letter, filled with ritual phrases at the top the way an aspirin bottle is stuffed with cotton wool: Thanks very much for your letter. It will take us quite some time to review it. It will have to go to the board but please be advised Disney will not end on this, we will actively promote our interests worldwide. Lots of love, etc.

It was a Dear John letter. But it wasn't even a good Dear John letter. When guys at the battlefront during a war get a Dear John, at least they know their wife or girlfriend has found someone else and isn't going to wait for them. It's agonising, but at least it frees them to get on with their life. This Disney version didn't free us to do anything. It kept us suspended in aspic. It was effectively a non letter. I was hopping mad and threw it on the table. Francis retrieved it and re-read it.

'You know what's in it,' I said to him. 'Why're you reading it over and over?'

'I want to try and see if there is anything positive we could take out of it.'

'There isn't. Why would they hide positive stuff?'

Not even Francis could find as much as a crumb of consolation in that first letter. Nor in any of the letters which came over the ensuing months. He had to keep going like a cartoon figure with a ball and chain attached to their ankle. The next step was to prepare for Cannes in October 2000, with our good friends and allies, McConnells. We were doing a further demonstration of the DVD and giving out merchandising items. We brought boxes of t-shirts with Piggley

Pooh nicely embroidered on them. Ralph Lauren would have been proud of the quality of workmanship. They were specially printed on fabric and then sewn on. A wonderful woman named Mary from Kildare provided them and they were very much sought after by television executives at Cannes and Las Vegas.

The objective was that anyone who encountered us at Cannes would go away with something to remember us and the project by. If the person was Australian, we'd have Piggley Pooh done wearing the Australian hat with the corks dangling from it, and a Waltzing Matilda slogan underneath.

It's amazing how effective a communications tool a t-shirt or a soft toy can be. They can reinforce in the minds of potential purchasers the reality of an otherwise theoretical concept. In addition, they can give a solidity and scale to the operation behind the concept. Many of the people at Cannes that year assumed that Francis was bigger than Tyrone Productions.

Now, Moya Doherty and John McColgan, the people behind Tyrone, had taken a seven-minute intermission act from the Eurovision Song Contest staged at the Point in Dublin and turned it into a global phenomenon called *Riverdance*. Tyrone Productions is big. Really big. Yet, by dint of embroidered t-shirts and soft toys, Francis managed to convince people at the Cannes Film Festival that the two of us were bigger than Tyrone. He never claimed it. But when it was assumed, he didn't feel the need to kill off the assumption. It wasn't going to do John and Moya any harm, and it just might do us some good.

Bringing physical product support (meaning soft toys) with him helped. It was not something most people pitching films or TV programme ideas at Cannes had ever done. So, even though in reality Francis had nothing to offer, over and above what he'd already offered at several Cannes festivals, the fact that the big Irishman, when he arrived on this occasion, had with him a whole set of talking animals – all branded with Piggley Pooh – created the illusion of something new.

It was not complete illusion. It was added value. Mary from Kildare was now hired to make clothes for more soft toys: pigs and ducks and hens. Once dressed in the distinctive costumes worn by the characters in the proposed series, these soft toys moved from being generics into being branded demonstrations of the onward march of the project.

Everywhere we went, we haunted toyshops and novelty stores. Francis spotted a little pig that snorted when he was on one of his overseas trips. When you squeezed it, it would make pig sounds. He could scarcely restrain himself from squeezing pig noises out of it in the plane on the way home. Most businessmen spend a fortune overseas on electronics and gizmos. Francis was spending buttons on soft toys and glowing with enthusiasm over the fact that you could make them snort to order.

As soon as Francis or I would pick up a toy representing any of the animals in the stories, I would bring it to Clane in Kildare, where Mary would make another jacket with Piggley Pooh on it or make a little coat for the cow or a hat for Henrietta hen or a shirt for Daniel the duck.

A seamstress in Clane was serving as wardrobe mistress for a planned TV series, and I was dresser to the stars. I could get a soft squishy Piggley into a new jacket in two seconds flat, and then allow Francis to go into his spiel at Cannes: 'This is how the toys will look when the series is made. Their appearance is all based on our animation series …'

One of the great appeals this had was that it was unexpected. Of course, it was unexpected because the Fitzpatricks were doing things completely the wrong way around. If Warner Brothers or Disney were setting out to make an animated series, they would have the stories, stars and animators all lined up before they even thought about merchandise. Series first, product later. We, on the other hand, had product although we had no series.

But that product gave Francis a confidence and a presence unjustified by the realities. A few squishy toys became the outward manifestation of a Big Claim.

'I had a platform,' he remembers. 'I had a US television customer. Not the biggest station in the world, but still, an arm of PBS that had shown Barney in his early days, that had shown Teletubbies before they became an international brand – this arm of PBS was genuinely interested in our series. Plus I had this merchandise and I had my Piggley Pooh clothing.'

Everybody else was at Cannes to sell or to buy. We were there to spin. No more, no less. Francis' main objective was to spin the world of television that everything was fine with us, we were just waiting for Disney to settle and wasn't it fantastic that the great Disney corporation saw such potential in our little pig that they were investing such time and money and expertise to halt his progress? And what was your name again? (Because Francis always liked to follow up by sending the person something personalised – believing, rightly, that it greatly enhanced the person's recollection of us and of our series.)

Behind the brave façade and the busy props supporting it, lay the realisation that taking on Disney could be a life sentence. I'd seen Erin Brokovitch and knew some of the tactics that Big Business had used against her and the people for whom she was fighting. It was a welcome distraction when, that autumn, I fell pregnant again. I was delighted about it, as was Francis. It didn't stop me ringing Francis at the office for updates though.

'Denise,' he would say, patiently, 'you know I'd've called you the minute a major development happened.'

'I just thought there might be a *minor* development.'

'Disney don't do minor developments.'

'But there must be *some* progress?'

'Denise, nothing is going to rush Disney. A big corporation is always going to take something like this to the twenty-fourth hour.'

Francis was probably lucky that so much of my time was absorbed by the children, the new pregnancy and supervising the building of our house in Skryne. We had managed to wrest planning permission from the local authority but getting the mortgage had been a huge problem. Given our general indebtedness and lack of progress in reducing it, asking a bank for a mortgage was a bit like standing on the rim of a live volcano while trying to get accident insurance. Bankers looked at us as if we were certifiable: 'Please,' their expressions said. 'Please go away quietly. Do not embarrass yourselves or us by pursuing this.'

I refused to accept the message of their expressions. Finance, to me, is a side-issue. I had a growing family who were, in my view, entitled to a great childhood, which meant a decent home. You can't postpone childhood, and there was no way I was going to postpone building my dream family home. Therefore, even after we had been refused mortgages by three or four banks, we kept going.

Just before Francis' fortieth birthday, we met Pauric Brennan, manager at the Bank of Ireland in Navan. He brought us into the commercial department of the Navan branch. We sat there, smiling grimly. The figures didn't add up. The commercial guy was very pleasant but very noncommittal. Pauric Brennan was doing his best for us: 'Look, these people are achievers,' he said earnestly. 'They haven't achieved yet but it's only a matter of time.'

We were touched by his efforts on our behalf, but the commercial guy didn't seem to be. I looked at the commercial guy square on: 'Whether you give us the loan or not is inconsequential,' I told him, heading for the door. 'Because – one way or the other – our builder starts work on Monday.'

Francis shrugged and followed me, trying not to laugh at the idea that we were going to go ahead with building the house with no money. He thought I'd shown great strength of character. The only thing he dreaded was the strength of character *he'd* have to show when it came to persuading a builder to start work without money.

Afterwards, I heard Francis on the phone trying to calm the bank people down.

'Look, we are waiting for replies from some of the other banks,' he was saying.

Yeah, I thought. They've already replied in the negative, but maybe if we wait long enough they'll reply again, positively this time.

'But we have the builders coming,' Francis went on.

Well, that's true, anyway.

'We're starting because we are going to get this mortgage from somebody,' he continued.

Hey, we haven't even made a tentative approach to the Mafia, yet.

'Yes, I appreciate you'd be surprised by what Denise said. Usually Denise and I would consult on something like that. But she was so frustrated because she knew we were going away and we needed a decision reasonably quickly, you know?'

When he came off the phone, I lit into him.

'Francis, we don't need any old decision. We need a "Yes" and we need it right now, not "reasonably quickly".'

'Denise, there's a good chance we've blown the whole thing.'

'You mean *I've* blown the whole thing.'

'Sometimes persuasion takes longer than you're willing to devote to it.'

'And sometimes we have nothing to lose,' I retorted.

On Francis' fortieth birthday, our banker rang to give us the approval we hadn't thought we'd get. We were thrilled. I suppose he so rarely had good news to communicate to us, he felt like making the extra effort to deliver this particular bit of joy fairly quickly. He certainly made the fortieth birthday celebrations much more positive and happy.

As my pregnancy drew on, our home began to take shape. Both of them satisfactory processes for me. Francis was having much less fun. He had to keep a flow of documentation going to the bankers to keep them off our back. If we counted them up – and we never had the time to – he probably wrote seventy-four different business plans. They were all the *same* business plan but they kept having to change. For our existing bankers, data had to go in to indicate that our market was expanding all the time. For new potential investors, the documents had to be angled differently.

We applied to Irish multimillionaire businessmen like J. P. McManus and Dermot Desmond. Every application took effort and time. Just one business plan, if you go to an accountancy firm for it, will cost you about £10,000. Francis did them all himself. If he wasn't so expert and so diligent, we could have spent £740,000 paying someone else to do that work – assuming we had that kind of money, which of course, we didn't.

Inevitably, the time Francis spent on churning out this paperwork reduced the time he could devote to his own legal practice.

I should have been worried sick and I should have been living in Francis' ear with my worries. But I've always had happy pregnancies, and during the time before George's birth, I was so enmeshed in getting the house built without it causing too much disruption to Klaragh and Daniel that I left Francis alone on the Piggley Pooh front. For the most part. Now and then I would send a shot across his bows, and he tolerated it. It suited him just as well for Miss Impatience not to be breathing down his neck and fussing him about details.

While venture capitalists proved to be largely a waste of his time, he'd also been talking to McConnells, our long-term advertising agency partners, seeking to persuade them to buy a shareholding in Piggley Pooh. Francis was making the point to them that this was going to a great opportunity for them to get in at this level before we got in the other contracts. They agreed and bought a five per cent stake in it. At that time, the two of us held one hundred per cent equity in it. Their investment was a very helpful injection because it gave the company a monetary value for bank purposes.

It wasn't the only positive for Piggley Pooh. Three strands were developing together that autumn. One was Mondo, the big Italian producers we were talking with. One was PBS in the US. The third was McConnells.

Even though the black cloud of Disney was still looming over us, and despite the fact that we were probably going to end up in the European Court sometime in the New Year, we had a sense that the stone was starting to roll. McConnells had demonstrated confidence in us and in Piggley Pooh, plus, it was a nice injection of capital, although we didn't actually get the money in one lump. In fact, no monies changed hands until March 2001; the capital transfer was dependent on the production going ahead. But, coming to the end of 2000, although Disney might have believed they had us immobilised, we were actually moving forward.

We were talking to Mondo Television, the largest Italian producers of animation. Francis had initiated contact with Ricki Corradi in Cannes in April 1999 and had kept building on their initial interest. They could envisage a deal with us which could be quite prestigious because Mondo are quoted on both the London and Italian stock markets.

'Why don't you raise 481 finance?' Francis suggested to them. 'Then bring it to the market and your share price will go up. You'll have a fifty per cent joint venture with us which will cost you nothing.'

A group of investors in the UK were also interested at that time.

Meanwhile, progress was happening in the US as a result of the encounter Francis had with Len Giarruputo the very first time we went to Cannes.

Len required to be paid. Not a huge amount, to Francis' way of thinking. His retainer was only £1,500 a quarter. *Only?* I certainly didn't think that was a small amount of money. Back in July 1998, we had met him in New York when we were over for a wedding. We were sitting in the lobby of the Crown Plaza and Francis had just asked me to go easy on the spending: 'We just can't afford to be lashing out money,' he told me.

I was resentfully absorbing this when in walked big Len Giarruputo. Out of his pocket Francis took a great wad of cash to hand to him. It was all I could do not to reach over, snatch it and run to the nearest Gap. But I controlled myself. Up to a point. Francis was talking to Len. All positive. All non-specific.

'Hallmark are strong on this,' Len said. 'Their VP, Richard Buchanan, in charge of children's programming, likes the concept a lot. Francis, you must come play golf with him sometime.'

'Look, Len,' I interrupted. 'What do you actually have for us?'

A stunned silence followed this eruption.

'When are we going to get real reports?' I went on. 'We need action. We need to know when we're actually going to have a television series.'

Francis opened his mouth to speak. I cut across him.

'How are we going to measure your success?' I asked Len.

Another silence. I just stared at him fiercely, because I had realised that we were paying this guy good money and I could not see what, if anything, we were getting in return. Actions speak louder than words to me and there seemed to be a lot more words than action. I know how it's done. I know you have to review what you're doing. I accept there have to be meetings. I may not have the sophisticated spreadsheet thinking of an international financier but I know damn well when no results are coming in. Cash, which was in such short supply that Francis was lecturing me about not using it, was being given to this man in a solid brick of banknotes and I wanted to see results for it. Now.

'Denise, we're getting results,' Francis said. 'Len's getting us results. He's established links with PBS – yes, I know they haven't been copperfastened yet, but he's getting us in the door.'

'Links,' I spat out. 'We can't take links to the bank. We're paying cash out all the time and –'

'Of course Len is getting cash from us,' Francis said, 'but he can get cash from other people as well.'

As far as Francis was concerned, even getting an agent was a step forward and his priority was to keep this man on board. Especially since Len – a major figure in the American entertainment business for decades – had, against his better judgement, taken us on despite us not having what Len regarded as the most basic pre-requisite for selling an animation project: a pilot film with high production values. Francis had always felt validated by Len's fatherly interest in him.

I could see he was – at this point – really bothered by my being so direct with Len, so I subsided and let him do more of the positive small-talk that had driven me to interrupt in the first place. Himself and Len picked up the way a family would pick up at a summer picnic having been interrupted by a mad bumble bee: now we've got that out of the way, where were we?

I watched the two of them, torn between the desire to hit Francis over the head with a chair and the urge to hug him. Hit him because he was engaged in what I saw as total bullshit. Hug him because I was beginning to realise that TV and film are ninety-five per cent bullshit and I have a complete bullshit deficit. That's where I would fail, particularly in an industry like entertainment, without my husband.

He is brilliant at working through tedium and easing a result out of waffle. I like things to be direct. I wanted directness applied, right now, to Len. Enough of this mushy warm relationship-building, was my view, let's cut to the chase, get to the bottom line, show some results.

'But to move that philosophy into the television industry is an impossibility,' Francis said after Len had gone. 'This whole industry involves people contact and building up relationships – it's a people business and a relationship business – there's no product without people and if you take away the limousines and the helicopters and the yachts in Cannes, which are all expenses-based, there's nothing there.'

'I seem to remember you telling me that Len asked you some awfully blunt questions the first time you met him in Cannes. He wanted to know the title, how many episodes, target audience, what the genre was. He called you "sonny boy" and indicated you weren't at the races.'

'But then he took me on. Took us on. Took the project on.'

'Big of him. We're paying him good money.'

'And he has introduced us to people who are going to broadcast our series when we get it made. Smacking Len around the head isn't going to get the series produced, Denise, satisfactory though it may be to you at the time.'

All I could do was laugh and agree to be kept away from

Len in the short term, lest I sink my teeth in his throat in a moment of impatience. I do firmly believe that the unspoken threat of 'Denise's-teeth-in-your-throat' was helpful to Francis in dealing with a lot of people though. Never consciously planned between us, our instinctive good cop/bad cop positions allowed Francis to be Mr Nice Guy. Sympathy for being married to a woman who's perceived to be tough can be a great advantage to a man.

That said, Francis also has the unusual ability of being able to make the hard decisions while still holding on to his friendship with he people negatively affected by those decisions. He works very hard to make it clear to people that while he may oppose a *policy*, it doesn't mean he's against the *personality* advancing that policy. He stays on their side even though a project or aspect of a project may fail. That has proved a benefit to us and it's something I admire greatly in him.

And Len *was* making important links for us. He had started introducing Francis to PBS in New York back in December 1998. Later he would meet the PBS team in Cannes.

PBS is made up of 360 stations, of which the one operated by Tom Salmon is the fourth largest. The American equivalent of the BBC, it had a lot of clout. *Barney* and *Teletubbies* had both started on regional stations, *Barney* in Connecticut. If we could develop product to give them, they were willing to offer a platform which would allow endless possibilities ... If Disney ever freed us up to put our pig on that platform.

Chapter Seventeen

MAY IT PLEASE THE COURT ...

Forget Hollywood. Don't even think about Meath. That winter of 2000, we thought of one location and one location only: Alicante, in Spain.

That's where the European Court is based, and that's where it looked as if we were going to have to move in order to work on the case. The idea was that we would all move over there for the duration. Francis. Me. The children. Francis envisaged the ultimate media circus, with him and me and the kids facing the press and saying 'Look what Disney, who are supposed to be all about children, are doing to us.'

At this point, we knew we had to face them head on. But the most frustrating part of that was they kept asking for a delay on the closing dates. The fact that they kept succeeding in their requests was interpreted by me as a really bad sign. I took it as indicating Disney's ability to manipulate the court to give them extra time. What enraged me was that they so clearly had no need for extra time. The case had not thrown up any extraordinary new issues during 2000, so why, after all the delays they had already wished on us, were they stretching it out even further? Of course, the answer to me was obvious: they hoped to drive us into bankruptcy so they would never have the trouble, expense or exposure of facing us in court.

Francis, on the other hand, was saying 'they are entitled, there is a certain statutory time limit they can have'. I knew he was working closely with McLachlan and Donaldson while at the same time trying to keep the conduit to Steve Ackerman open, because at the back of both of our minds was the belief that if we could kick sense into Ackerman, he would kick sense into Michael Eisner, the ultimate Disney boss man.

Two options exist for the parties in a dispute going before the European trademark court in Alicante. One is a full oral hearing. That didn't really suit Disney because the last thing they wanted was a family who had to leave their own country to go and defend their honour in Spain. While it would have been a huge plus for us and Francis was advised by McLachlan Donaldson from a media point of view that it would be explosive television and we would certainly get public sympathy all over Europe, nonetheless, how were we going to fund being down there?

In the course of doing the daunting sums on moving our entire family to Alicante, we realised that we would also, in the event of a full oral hearing, have to take our trademark specialists with us, too, particularly Norman McLachlan. If we needed him there, we would have to pay him on a daily basis: £3/4,000 a day, plus expenses. The concept of a full oral hearing, so attractive before the pocket calculators came out, began to look markedly less attractive.

As it turned out, the element of choice was taken out of our hands. No oral hearing happened, in the end, but both parties had to agree on that in advance. We agreed, but we were scared because this was being done behind closed doors. David and Goliath is a scenario that plays best in public, not in private. A serious judgement was going to be made, a decision that could mean the enabling of everything or the crumbling of everything. We had investors who were willing to take a risk to a certain point, but they wanted to wait for the judgement to come in before they irrevocably committed themselves to large scale expenditure.

The pleadings closed in the second week in January of 2001; all final submissions and arguments had to be made by then. Thereafter, the case would take its place in the list and we had no idea how soon it would be – it might be three months, it might be six.

Having agreed, and submitted the last of our legal submissions, we were back in Limbo again. In the spring, because we were due to meet Ricki from Mondo in the US, we decided, while we were there, to make one more attempt to get through to Steve Ackerman and, through him, to the bosses at Disney Inc. As already recounted (Chapter One) this telephone confrontation was enormously satisfying – emotionally – but of no use whatever in moving Disney towards a civilised buyout of our rights to the name Pooh.

We flew home from the US in a mood of almost serene surrender to the worst. We had done our best and had met with the arrogant intransigence of a vast corporation used to crushing impertinent would-be competitors like paper crisps in a bag. Having rattled them with our last attempt at reconciliation, they would undoubtedly pursue us with all the resources at their disposal, fuelled by rage. Our character, our project, our future and even the faint possibility of long-term solvency were in the hands of a court based in Spain whose members had never seen us or heard us talk, and who, we greatly feared, could be overwhelmed by the money-driven legal might of Disney.

Weeks passed, and with their passing came the gradual, inevitable shift of the Alicante judgement from front of the mind to – if not the back of the mind – somewhere other than the top of our mental agendas.

Then one spring morning, Francis was driving down Raglan Road and thought it would be a lovely place to stop to eat the lunch he had brought with him. It was a sunny April day. Just as he was tidying away the remnants of his meal, the mobile phone rang. It was Peter McLachlan, our trademark expert: 'Francis? It's Peter.'

'Hi, Peter.'

Francis was scanning Raglan Road looking for a rubbish container. He thought Peter's call was likely to be routine, because he phoned quite regularly just to give Francis any information he had because he knew how desperately Francis was waiting for it.

'It's coming through,' Peter said, with great excitement.

'How do you mean, coming through?' asked Francis, giving up the search for the garbage container.

'On the fax.'

'*What's* coming through?'

'The judgement. From Alicante.'

Francis' hand squashed the bag of debris into a couple of square inches of solidity.

'What is it? What's the judgement?'

'I haven't read it.'

'You mean you don't know if we've won or not?'

'It's coming through *now*.'

Francis could hear the fax machine in the background, churning out the pages that would kill us or cure us.

'You won, you won!'

Peter's voice was more excited than Francis had ever heard.

'But the fax is still working,' Francis said.

'Yes, but the last page came out first,' Peter laughed. 'It was a one line judgement. Sorry, what I mean is it's a one line finale but it was one of the longest judgements in the trademark court – the cover sheet says it's twenty-five pages.'

At this point, Francis, the eternal optimist, lost his optimism. He was afraid to relax into Peter's wonderful news.

'How sure are you, Peter?'

'The last page says the objection is overruled, the applicant is entitled to registration as the owner of the trademark.'

'We're the applicant, right?'

'Of course. The objector was Disney. And here's more good news, Francis –'

'Yes?'

'Costs were awarded to the applicant. You won your costs. You're covered.'

Disney had been hammered. The judge in Alicante had said 'NO. End of story.'

Francis forced himself to be enthusiastic, to convey the enthusiasm he knew he should be feeling, and stress the gratitude we both owed to Peter and his father. When the phone clicked off, though, he sat there, numbed with relief. Then he lifted it again and speed-dialled me. I started to tell my parents, who were in the room with me, passing on what he was saying while he was saying it, and then trying to hear the next thing he said over their whoops of delight and congratulations.

'Francis, you're brilliant.'

'Denise, we won.'

'We did. We won. I can't believe it.'

'Me neither.'

'But you know something, Francis? We deserved to win. Congratulations. You coming home now?'

The minute I asked the question, I could have answered it in the negative. Of course Francis would go round first to the offices of our trademark agents to thank them for their skill, their commitment and their endless patience over the years. At home, I felt as if I could fly. All the setbacks and postponements meant nothing now. The decision coming in like that, so unequivocal, so clear, was brilliant. It was exciting, but above all it was a great relief.

Francis may have been filled with more courage than sense when he told Ackerman the sum he was demanding and further instructed Ackerman never to telephone him directly again, but to get his boss, Eisner, to make any future calls. Now, a short few weeks after that phonecall, we could not help wonder if Ackerman and Eisner shouldn't have taken Francis up on the offer and at least gone a little further down the road to a closure which would have left the Fitzpatricks solvent and with some hope of a future for Piggley Pooh.

They had lost the trademark battle. They had lost it unequivocally in the European Court. There could, of course, be an appeal. That would have rankled with Disney. But what was arguably worse for the family-entertainment giant was the gloss put on our victory by international media. Typical was the *London Sunday Times* of 24 June (exactly one month, to the day, before our second son, George, was born). Here's how their reporter, Jan Battles, put it:

IRELAND'S PIGGLEY POOH
PUTS DISNEY TO SHAME
Piggley Puffs Disney Away

An Irish couple is set to earn millions from a cartoon character called Piggley Pooh after winning a court battle against Disney Enterprises over copyright.

Denise Fitzpatrick, a 35 year old housewife from County Meath, and her husband, Francis, have landed a four-year television deal in America. The Adventures of Piggley Pooh will be broadcast to almost fifty million American homes from September 2002.

Hailed as the next Teletubbies, the cartoon is expected to generate up to $5 billion in sales of merchandise.

Having battled for years against Disney over the pig's surname, the couple can now proceed with the series. Disney claimed it held the rights to the name Pooh, since it owned the trademark Winnie the Pooh.

The Meath couple's series tells the story of Piggley Pooh, a fun-

loving pig who lives with his family and friends on a rustic farmyard at the foot of the Hill of Tara in Meath. A storyteller, Piggley Pooh recounts tales based on Celtic folklore such as the Salmon of Knowledge and the Children of Lir as well as international adventure stories.

Francis Fitzpatrick, 41, a media and entertainment lawyer, has spent recent weeks finalising deals to Piggley Pooh with television stations and toy companies in America and Britain. The toy licence, worth an estimated 3m to 5m alone, is being sought by Hasbro and Mattel, two of the biggest manufacturers in the world.

The Fitzpatricks have had to wait six years to see Piggley Pooh make it to the screen. In 1995, soon after his wife began creating stories based on the cartoon pig. Fitzpatrick registered Piggley Pooh as a trademark in Ireland. When he went to register it Europe-wide in 1998, Disney objected and sued him in the European Trademark Court in Alicante, Spain.

Disney maintained that the Fitzpatricks' pig infringed its rights to Winnie the Pooh, the bear created by A. A. Milne.

'They claimed ownership to the word Pooh and said there would be too much of a conflict between our character and their character,' said Fitzpatrick.

Winnie the Pooh is Disney's most popular personality, generating about $6 billion in retail sales a year.

The case took four years to go through the court, during which time the couple faced bankruptcy.

'It was David versus Goliath's big brother,' said Fitzpatrick. 'We had no chance of winning against the Disney corporation. It was a ten million to one shot, but we always had hope. It was an impossible dream. Everybody told us to give up.'

Our own local paper, the Meath Chronicle, noted that it was when the judgement came through that investors who had been waiting in the wings came forward with deals that will ultimately put Piggley Pooh on TV screens all over America and further afield. It quoted Francis saying that if it hadn't been for my parents, James and Maura, his own, Frank and Patricia, and other members of our families, we would never have got through.

The stories carried by media near home were picked up and run by media far away, so that a long-lost cousin telephoned our home from New Zealand, asking my father if the Denise mentioned in the stories and pictured in most of them was his daughter. He was very happy to confirm that I was. So it reunited our extended family.

In fact, by 25 July 2001, when George was born, he arrived into a family famous all over the world for taking on and beating a major international entertainment corporation. He didn't seem that pushed about it, though.

From Disney, there was no contact. They never complained. They never explained. They never commented. They never congratulated us. There was a deafening silence.

Eventually, the cheque for costs came through, although unfortunately the trademark costs are not like legal costs. We were due only about €1,000. Francis never collected the cheque from McLachlan Donaldson. He keeps meaning to ask whatever happened to it, because it would be a nice souvenir just to have a cheque from Disney.

He'll certainly never cash it now.

What surprised us was how widespread was the delight at our taking Disney down a peg. You might expect that kind of response if a couple had won a battle against, say, Microsoft, which has a hard image, internationally. On the surface, Disney has a much softer image. But the aftermath of our litigation established that the soft surface image did not have depth.

What *did* have depth was a long-standing view of the corporation as punishing, greedy and merciless. This perception was held on both sides of the Atlantic. Disney had been in litigation with the Sleisinger family for almost thirty years over ownership of Pooh, and every single person who Disney had come up against – whether it was the A. A. Milne estate, Disney's son, Robin Moon, or his daughters – had been crushed. For all of those who had been crushed by Disney, this was a moral victory. A hugely satisfying moral victory.

Within the television industry, it was greeted as an heroic feat. No individual had given such a bloody nose to a large corporation. It was front page news across the globe and to this day Francis is greeted in TV circles with extra enthusiasm and introduced as 'the guy who succeeded against Disney'.

Celebrations broke out in Meath and ran for two or three weeks outright. Those celebrations weren't triumphalist. Or perhaps it would be more honest to say that they weren't *just* triumphalist. They also registered the fact that Alicante had put us in a very good position with the investors. We knew we had brought the project creatively anyway to where we could have brought it. Now we were going to be able to make the series because the investors who had been interested all along, now felt it was safe to take the brakes off their investment and really go for it.

'Easy for them,' I said to Francis with our new baby in my arms. 'If it hadn't worked out the way it did, the investors who are so eager and gung-ho now wouldn't have lost anything. We took all the risk.'

'You can't think of those things,' Francis said. 'You have to go ahead and decide on the business, how we're going to get the series made. And made to a high standard, because we've pitched a high quality product to PBS.'

That was certainly true. It was the first time in the history of television as a medium that Ireland had developed programming for children which was deeply rooted in the oral Irish tradition but aimed at the American market – and, in due course, at the rest of the world.

Chapter Eighteen

PIGGLEY'S SLICE OF FAME

Here's an amazing thought. Amazing to me, anyway. Even as you read my words in the book in front of you, hundreds of thousands of children, somewhere in America, Australia, the UK, Ireland and a number of countries worldwide, are seeing my concept on their televisions.

Once the giant lost the battle with us, we were media heroes. The character of the storytelling pig we had developed and fought for was as famous as we were, because most of the stories included pictures of Piggley, glasses on his snout, book in hand, ready to start telling stories. Our agent, Len Giarruputo had won an agreement in principal out of WLIW 21 that it would broadcast the series. TV stations all over the world were now interested in following suit.

At NATPE, the big gathering of the North American Television market, held in Las Vegas at the end of January, Francis was lionised. He was there with the Irish Enterprise Board, which provides funding for people in Ireland producing television material to sell their wares overseas.

We were surrounded by boosters and willing partners. Mondo, the Italian TV producers we'd been meeting the night of the Algonquin telephone call, were doubly delighted when we beat Disney. They were glad because they saw it as opening up for them the possibility of making the series, probably using some of the Section 481 financing Francis had talked to them about.

A second reason they were chuffed by our victory was that they themselves had had some difficulties with Disney, who had reached out across the ocean to warn them off taking liberties with *Cinderella*, *Beauty and the Beast* or *Sleeping Beauty*. Each of these had been in the public domain for centuries, but a threat from Disney, claiming ownership of them, tended to shrivel the confidence of competing corporations.

Only naïve enthusiasts like us, or dog-determined power figures like Michael Moore, were stimulated into greater defiance by a threat from the Magic Kingdom. When Disney pulled out of a distribution deal with Moore, believing that his movie, *Fahrenheit 9/11*, was too close to the Republican bone, Moore threw what amounted to a profitable global tantrum.

Week after week went by while he negotiated another distributor for his damning documentary about President Bush. He was never out of the headlines, never done rubbishing the Disney company for its craven caving in to the demands of its powerful friends. By the time the movie opened, it was an international talking point and on the first day, the queues for the cinemas showing it stretched as far as the queues for the premiere of a Harry Potter movie. Until *Spiderman* knocked it off its perch, Moore's film was the most popular film in America.

That was some achievement for a documentary, and some of the credit has to go to Disney for giving it publicity it could never, in the normal run of things, have hoped for.

Mondo, having had their own troubles with Disney, were dying to get going with us. Ricki Corradi, one of the family running that company, enjoyed every contact with Francis. The feeling was mutual. Francis loved Corradi's flamboyance, admired his skill in martial arts and appreciated his discipline, when he needed it. His brother, Matteo, handles the finance for the group, which has a strong relationship with an important Korean producer. Ricki wanted half of Piggley Pooh, worldwide.

Piggley had come out of the Disney deep-freeze in better shape than when he'd gone in. Now, when we knocked on doors, those doors opened. To open the final door to the millions which would accrue from, say, selling toys in every branch of Toys R Us, all we needed was product. To be precise, we needed twenty-six episodes of Piggley doing his animated thing. Making twenty-six episodes of high quality animation would cost $10m and change. We had the change but not the $10m.

Francis had assiduously kept in touch with both Goodbody Stockbrokers, which is owned by AIB, and Davy Stockbrokers, which is owned by Bank of Ireland, throughout the battle with Disney. They had all promised that as soon as the case was resolved, seven, ten, even as much as thirty million dollars could be raised in Dublin. Now, with the case resolved and a portfolio of positive coverage from the international media in his hand, Francis pitched up on their doorsteps but found that these guys had been peddling dreams.

They may have believed what they had been telling Francis, but they should not have believed such wannabe hypothetical hope-spinning. The financial reality, as Francis quickly understood, was that they couldn't raise one pound in Dublin. Not a pound. Not a euro. Not a dollar.

No Irish bank had the expertise. No Irish bank had the specialist understanding that comes from investment in television and movies. All they could ever offer was Section 481 investments which would only give ten per cent of any budget. They were just touting for business which they would pass on to specialist banks in London – Warburg Pinkus or Barclays Film Finance. So, from the day of the judgement, 21 April 2001, we had until 21 June to get investors on board because that was the window within which Disney had to appeal.

Francis went through meeting after fruitless meeting with stockbrokers in Davy's and Goodbodys and Merrion Capital.

He had Ricki Corradi of the Corradi family on his back about their investment. It came down to the following: the Corradi family were offering $250,000 payment to us plus 50/50 joint venture going forward. A London-based group of investors, led by an Irish businessman from Entara Limited, was offering us £350,000 sterling as a payment and then a 50/50 venture going forward. At the end of the day we went with the English team. They impressed us because they accepted they knew nothing about the animation industry. They would finance it and leave Francis as chairman to bring the project forward. We signed up with them on 16 May 2001.

Disney, meanwhile, lodged no appeal within the period of time at their disposal. The project began to move from neutral to first gear, and for almost the first year, everything went as planned. After about nine months, the Royal Bank of Scotland were brought in because while Entara Limited were prepared to put up a certain amount of money, they needed to finance that by a combination of other people's equity or bank finance. They succeeded in putting a package together which at the end of the day raised $24m.

By October 2001, we were in Cannes together. Following Francis' guidance they hired the right studio: Mike Young, based in Los Angeles. They then went with Francis to PBS to meet the affiliate, WLIW 21 New York. Francis had obviously achieved a hell of a deal because all they had to do was expand from PBS regional into PBS Central, i.e. to convince PBS to go national. So they decided to move ahead and make the series.

In March 2002, Royal Bank of Scotland threw a major wobbly. They decided that Disney were too dangerous in the marketplace and that 'Pooh' must come out of the Piggley Pooh name. Otherwise, went their theory, the minute we launched our series, Disney could swamp every transmitting area with *Winnie the Pooh* at loss-leader pricing. We would be squeezed out of the market since Disney could beat us in price every time.

The bank's stance was that we weren't even going to get product into the marketplace because the Disney guys would say to any station using a lot of Disney products: 'it's them or us.' Bank of Scotland would not put its investors or itself in a situation where they could, as they saw it, be blown out of the water before the series even started.

We were back to square one. Square one is bad enough on your first visit, but it's no joy at all when you have to go back after half a decade of fighting. But Francis gamely picked up the battle.

Mike Young, one of the best producers of children's animation in the US, went along with Bank of Scotland. He was convinced that using the Pooh name would only antagonise Disney. Mike asked other people in the industry to advise us independently and most of them were of the opinion that the Pooh name was not essential to the success of the character.

I remained unconvinced. Francis was in a very difficult situation. He wanted to support me but knew the investors would not continue with the investment if we did not change the name. Matters came to a head when we attended a board meeting in Bond Street at the head offices of Entara, the London Irish investors, and ourselves, in October 2002.

At that meeting a number of the senior directors and executives were present. One of the directors opened stating that they had canvassed about fifty investors and at least as many banks. All were of the opinion that if we persisted with the name Pooh that Disney would come after us and at worst block the series or delay it. This was a risk that neither the banks nor the investors were prepared to take; Royal Bank of Scotland stating bluntly that unless we changed the name they would pull out.

The attitude of investors and banks seemed to me very cowardly. Had we not a European Court judgement in our favour which said we owned the name Piggley Pooh? Or is European law not worth the paper it's written on?

I was shaken to the very core. You can beat these bad guys in court, you can win against impossible odds and then, low and behold, they win anyway, because bankers and investors go cautious on you. Had the whole European justice system melted in front of the might of an American dragon? I dug my heels and everything else in. The lady was not for turning whether Royal Bank of Scotland, the investors, Mike Young the producer, and the whole shagging lot of them, including my husband, were against me.

The board meeting ended and Francis and myself were chauffeured in the Entara car back to Heathrow Airport. In absolute silence.

It may seem a small thing to change the name of a character. However, having fought tooth and nail over five years and three continents, I was not prepared to see it as a small thing. I did, however, begin to do some silent soul-searching over the next day or two, with Francis steering clear of me, knowing I was in turmoil as I grappled with the very deep problem of the Pooh name and that only I could come to terms with it.

Francis came home after one of his trips to Britain to try to get the issue sorted and, glancing out of the window as he was getting out of the car, it struck me that he looked the way I imagine policemen look when they have to come to someone's front door to tell them that a relative of theirs has been killed in a car crash. When he came in the door, I went to him, feeling miserable for what I was putting him through.

'Francis, let me just get this clear. We beat Disney, right?'

He nodded.

'We didn't beat them in Ireland, we beat them in *Europe*?'

Another nod.

'They didn't appeal?'

A shake of the head.

'They couldn't have been *more* in the wrong?'

Back to nods.

'Yet they're so big and powerful that fear of Disney is forcing Royal Bank of Scotland to abandon what we won? Voluntarily?'

Another silent nod. I looked at him, the shape of him gone wobbly as my eyes filled up with tears.

'So even though Disney lost, in a sense they won?'

Francis came over to me and put his arms around me.

'Did they?' he asked gently. 'Maybe we both won.'

As he straightened up, I banged the tears away with the back of my hand and looked a question at him.

'We've done very well out of it,' he said softly. 'If you hadn't called it Piggley Pooh in the first place, Disney would never have had a reason to fight with us. But without Disney, perhaps we had nothing. Just another tiny idea without any real hope. There's 5,000 new projects a year in animation. Two will make it. Those are the odds. And they won't really be commercial successes. Once every five years there's a commercial success. It looks as if Piggley Winks is going to be a commercial success. A big commercial success.'

'Piggley Whatdidyousay?'

'Piggley Winks.'

'Piggley *Winks*,' I said, in a voice loaded with contempt.

'Piggley WINKS,' Francis responded, giving it a different, more upbeat flavour.

Suddenly the two of us were laughing. If the pig had to be called anything other than Pooh, Winks was the best option. It had an engaging echo of the old children's game, *Tiddly Winks*. I felt that in loyalty, I shouldn't relinquish Pooh so easily. But who was I serving by dragging out my surrender? Especially when the only people who would suffer if I kicked up a ruckus about it were Francis, Klaragh, Daniel and George, our baby. My heart sunk but my head had to rule for now. I needed to put my children's needs before my own and my beloved Piggley Pooh.

'Piggley Winks it is,' I said.

Francis, in the months following, got on with making the family fortune. He had picked very well when he selected Mike Young's firm as animators. Mike has a string of hits in the US. His most famous one is *Clifford the Big Red Dog* which is on coast to coast. It's now gone through four series and a theatrical release. It's almost as big as *Rugrats*. Francis was convinced from the start that we needed a studio like that to take up Piggley Winks. His theory was that if you have a great boy band, you have a lot of talent that may stay anonymous and go nowhere, whereas if you have a great boy band and take it to Louis Walsh, there's a chance you will end up with Westlife or Boyzone. Similarly with U2, Paul McGuinness was the vital element for their long-term success. Mike Young would be essential for the success of Piggley Winks.

However, Francis is realistic enough to know that Mike Young didn't need Piggley Pooh (or Winks, as he now was) and was not likely to come on board unless he was extremely positive that something was going to happen. So, a couple of weeks after the European Court came through with their judgement, I saw Francis express-airmailing Mike a copy of the *Sunday Times* 'Disney floored by Denise' story. That has opened doors all over the world. The world is made up of two types of people – those who love Disney and those who hate them. We're the favourite sons and daughters of the latter. Thank you Disney, you've put us on the map, you terrorised us and you very nearly killed us but because we survived, we're now reaping the benefits.

Once Mike came on board, he began to use his superb contacts list, with the result that our own Richard Harris was lined up to do the voice of the grandfather pig. Sadly, Richard Harris, having become beloved of a young film audience because of his appearance in the Harry Potter movies, died unexpectedly. Just as he had appeared in the J. K. Rowling stories because his granddaughter asked him to, he wanted to do Piggley Pooh for her, too.

The same rationale came into play when Mel Brooks was asked by Mike Young to consider the role. He agreed – for his granddaughter – and took the role of Wylie the sheep. Older Hollywood stars seem to do animation for their kids or grandkids. It's a fun job. It's even great fun being involved in the publicity. It's just an all-round enjoyable job.

The animators managed to create a visual link to the new name, too: older Piggley winks when he's winding up a story. Kind of leaving it to you, the viewer, to decide whether this is fiction or fact. Each story has a moral in it, so there are a number of choices for the young viewer to make at the end of each episode. It's good.

Piggley Winks is owned by a group of London-based investors led by a successful Irish businessman in the IT sector from 'Entara Limited', with the Fitzpatricks holding 4.5 per cent. As its creator, I have roughly the sort of income I figure I'd now be making in Smurfits, if I'd stayed with them.

Our shareholding has so far generated payments which have enabled us to build the house of our dreams on Raloo Farm where Piggley Pooh lived and continues to live in my imagination. On its own, it's been tremendously successful and we're reasonably comfortable thanks to it.

But what it has done for us is more than earn us money, although after all the years of begging and borrowing (we drew the line at stealing) that, in itself, would have been enough. These days Francis has a number of projects, any one of which is at least as big as Piggley Winks. He would never have gotten next, nigh or near those projects without Piggley Winks, without going through the Disney crucible.

In addition, Francis has parlayed his experience during the years of fighting Disney into an unequalled expertise. He is now a celebrity entertainment lawyer with a special understanding of the international law surrounding intellectual copyright.

For me, the biggest kick comes from having taken the memories, lessons and legends of my own happy childhood and turned them into something which will be experienced by children who might never, otherwise, even have heard of Ireland. Ten, twenty or thirty years from now, a child who at this moment is mesmerised watching the older Piggley Winks telling the story of the Salmon of Knowledge will come to Ireland as a visitor, or perhaps as a student, because of the magic spell an animated TV series cast on him or her.

When we went into this, neither of us had been in the industry at all or knew anything about it. Everything we've learned, we've learned through experience – actually living it. No amount of telling you what you are going to face could ever prepare you for what we went through. We learned the hard way. We would now be very good advisors to anybody starting off.

When I ask Francis if he would do it again, his immediate body-language answer is a nod: 'I *am* doing it again but from a very different vantage point. A great vantage point. I now am sought out. I am the man who, in television terms, makes the impossible happen.'

One of those impossibilities is the show *Socca Stars*. Screen-time, the owners of *Popstars* worldwide, from Australia, and Francis, have collaborated to merge the entertainment of reality TV with 'The Premiership'. I don't even want to think about the complexities of trying to merge the football industry and television, but Francis has been hard at that for two years and owns twenty-five per cent of it simply because they wanted him as a member of their team – not only as a lawyer but as a negotiator. Francis' good friend Larry Bass, a successful Irish TV producer who is dad to four kids, is one of his partners on *Socca Stars*. In addition, Francis is a director of Larry's award-winning production company, Screentime Shinawil Limited, who produce Ireland's top-rated entertainment show, *You're a Star*.

Our operation in the St Stephen's Green Centre, from which all of this sprang, all those years ago, is still going strong, although it now operates under the name Bramblewood Creations. I'm planning to introduce new products, including personalised CDs and computer software, allowing the child to interact with the story on the computer screen in front of them. But even though I want to refresh our product line, the fact is that the market for our personalised books is as solid as ever. It's just phenomenal that eight years after we started that should be the case. We've added new titles at various points along the line, so that we now have twenty-eight titles in total. Every Christmas is better than the Christmas before.

The house we live in is 800 yards from where I grew up, observing the animals and telling myself stories. Our children are living the childhood I had. They're with animals all the time: a pony called Bracken, a cat called Ginger, and two dogs (a West Highland called Jock and a Labrador called Jill). In addition, there are cows and calves and horses all round them so they're actually living inside Piggley Winks' world and they're oblivious to it. They're innocent and that's the beauty of it all. That's what we have been able to give them, as a result of the money finally coming through from Piggley Winks, the series.

We had a lot of loans to pay back, but they're coming to

an end, now. We're out of the financial woods at this stage. Francis drives a Mercedes, I drive a top of the range Rangerover, we can afford to have a horse for Klaragh and stable it. Francis keeps talking about buying himself a horse, too, but I tell him we need to get the garden straight first.

'First time I said I wanted a horse, you said we needed to get the house straight first,' he complains. 'I sacrificed a horse for a stairs! The first time we were truly liquid, I said to myself, right, I'm going to buy myself a racehorse because that's what I've always wanted from being a little boy who was at school with the jockey Walter Swinburn who rode *Shergar* in the Epsom Derby in 1982, the year I was doing my final law exams! I always wanted my own racehorse. I had one organised, up to the day I got the bill for the staircase and found you'd gone for a bifurcating structure with stairs going in two different directions. I had to say: "forget the racehorse, I can't pay for both. I'll go with the bifurcating stairs …"'

When Francis spits out 'bifurcating' about the stairs like a swearword, I point out to him that you don't have to feed or muck out a staircase.

Sooner or later, though, Francis will buy himself a hunter. Plus, probably a racehorse. I love horse racing. I love the buzz of being there. I wouldn't mind a share in a horse. Some people like to sail, some people like to buy football clubs or support them, some people like to own racehorses. It's one of the dreams Francis and I would love to fulfil.

But, while we enjoy where we've reached, we never forget what we had to come through to get here: all the tribulations and trials and purgatory through which we managed to get to this good place we're in. That is thanks in no small part to the Disney corporation. Neither of us really holds any animosity towards them. We recognise that if they had not shone their light on us we wouldn't have grown.

The children understand that the series is ours, but really they don't understand – for them it's another TV programme. Our daughter, Klaragh, when we were fighting with Disney, would asked Francis why he was away all the time.

'Well sweetheart,' Francis told her, 'Disney, this big giant, is trying to take away our Piggley Pooh.'

Klaragh always had a little pink pig, a fluffy toy with Piggley Pooh on it. When the *Sunday Times* came to take our picture, Klaragh was photographed holding her pig and she kept saying to the photographer and the journalist: 'They're trying to kill my pig.'

It was heart-wrenching.

Best of all is the fact that what we came through, Francis and I, has made us closer. Everything. From the big scary legal encounters to the annoying minor events like Kinko's. We did it together. We survived it all and as a result of what we've come through, we know and trust each other so well. Even on the worst days, we were able to work together and come out the other end. We've always sorted it out. We never went to bed not speaking to each other following a fight. We never do long term sulks. The bad times were all short term. Intensive short term.

We did it. I'm proud we did it, and I'm glad it's over. It's a chapter in my life that's closed. I would have no interest in doing anything like that again. I'll support Francis in his TV projects but for me, the priority is a simple one: to give each of my five children a childhood as magical and sustaining as mine was.

It's up to each of them to find their own stories to tell about their own beloved pet animals …

ACKNOWLEDGEMENTS

I would like to thank all of those who reached out with helping hands along the way; not all are mentioned below but those who helped know who they are and they will always retain a warm place in my heart. Without you we could not have survived and with your wind at our back we climbed the terrifying mountain.

In no particular order I wish to thank :
Robert Ryan (a terrific lawyer, friend and brother-in-law), Brendan Heneghan, Manoj Chawla, Peter Howick, Alf Thornton, Dave Kelly, Ciaran Hickey, Cormac Lucy, Tony Nico, Brian Hamilton, Gerry McDonnell, Hugh Ward, David Moss, Anne Bannon, Niall and Joyce Sheerin, Miriam Peters, Arlene McIntyre, Sandra and Ken Sheridan, Bernie Hyland, Michael Dolan, Oliver and Katie Connolly, John Cheatle, Ronan Heever, Frank Lynch, Hugh Doyle, Eddie Morrissey, Michael Flynn, Rhyna McCarthy (our superb photographer), Frank Sheerin, Cardinal Cathal Daly, Fr Joe Gleason, Bunter Purcell, Damian Purcell, Killian and Julierna Kavanagh, Paul Dubsky, Kevin Linehan, Seamus Farrelly, my sisters (and their husbands) Derval, Emer, Kay, Carole, Joan, Sharon, my brothers Jimmy and Brian (and his wife, Deirdre), Francis' brothers and sisters, Patrick, Mary, Josephine, Daniel, Patricia, Kat, Seán (and their spouses), John Walsh, Barry Rothwell, Cathal Gaffney, Darragh O'Connell, Seamus Cashman, all our friends and relations in Skryne and Tara, and Gerard for all his support. I wish to remember my aunt, Molly, who died this year (after whom we named our baby girl), and my baby sister, Moya, who died in infancy. I also want to mention Francis' grandmother, May O'Beirne, who died in

1987 but who left Francis with a real appreciation of the Irish art of storytelling; she was a real seanchaí. Francis' friend, John Fay, who died tragically in 1988, has also been a real inspiration to him.

A very special thanks to my co-author, Terry Prone, for putting up with me – and for all the enthusiasm, good humour and energy that she contributes to all who are lucky enough to encounter her, she is brilliant.

A huge thank you to my parents, Maura and Jimmy Swan, and to Francis' parents, Patricia and Frank Fitzpatrick, we always knew you were with us in the front line.

Finally, thanks to everyone who, in their own unique way, helped us to fulfil our dreams, we never felt alone despite the intense heat of the battle.